DISCARDED

The Secret World War II

THE SECRET WORLD WAR II

DON LAWSON

FRANKLIN WATTS

New York | London | 1978

Photographs courtesy of:

Wide World Photos: pp. 2, 29, 32, 81, 87, 88, 90, 92; Library of Congress: p. 7;
Compton's Encyclopedia, photo by Bill Cassin: p. 15; U.S. Signal Corps: pp. 23,
51, 98; U.S. Navy: p. 42; U.S. Air Force: pp. 48, 57; U.S. Army Air Force: pp.
75, 109; Graphic Persuasion Inc., and Don Lawson: pp. 58 (top and bottom), 60
(top and bottom), 61, 96, 101.

Library of Congress Cataloging in Publication Data

Lawson, Don.
  The secret World War II.

  Bibliography: p.
  Includes index.
  SUMMARY: Discusses World War II espionage
activities including intelligence personnel, codes
and ciphers, and propaganda.
  1. World War, 1939–1945—Secret service—Juvenile
literature. [1. World War, 1939–1945—Secret service.
2. Espionage] I. Title.
D810.S7L33   940.54'86   77-21185
ISBN 0-531-01459-2

Copyright © 1978 by Don Lawson

All rights reserved
Printed in the United States of America
6 5 4 3

TO MY GREAT, GOOD FRIEND
R. W. "ROCK" CANNON,
WHO WAS ALWAYS THERE
WHEN THE WHISTLE BLEW
IN WORLD WAR II
—D.L.

Contents

The Mysterious Death of Admiral Yamamoto

On a crystal-clear tropical morning in the spring of 1943 at the peak of the fighting between the United States and Japan in the Pacific during World War II, two Japanese Mitsubishi twin-engined bombers approached Kahili airport on Bougainville Island to make a landing. The "Bettys," as the American flyers called the Mitsubishi bombers, were escorted by six Zero fighters manned by the top fighter pilots in the Japanese air force. Their role was to protect the Bettys, which were carrying extremely valuable human cargo: Admiral Isoroku Yamamoto, commander in chief of the Combined War Fleet of Japan, and his staff.

Admiral Yamamoto was one of Japan's great war heroes. He had planned the highly successful attack against the U.S. Pacific war fleet at Pearl Harbor, which started the war for the United States, as well as numerous other air strikes throughout the Pacific, including the one on Midway Island. On this day, April 18, 1943, he was scheduled to land on Bougainville on one leg of an inspection tour of Japanese bases. He and his staff had left the Japanese stronghold of Rabaul at dawn. Having flown the 300 miles (482 km) to Bougainville exactly on time—Yamamoto demanded strict punctuality in all operations—the Bettys and their

Japanese Admiral Isoroku Yamamoto,
whose plane was ambushed by American flyers
after the Japanese secret code was broken.

escorts were now preparing to set down at Kahili. The time was precisely 9:35 A.M.

And exactly at this moment sixteen U.S. Army twin-boomed P-38 Lightning fighter planes boiled out of the sun and, wing-guns blinking death and destruction, attacked the startled Japanese.

The free-for-all dogfight that followed lasted only a few moments. The results were devastating for the Japanese. Both Betty bombers were destroyed and their passengers killed. Four Zeroes were also shot down. Just one P-38 Lightning failed to return from this murderously successful American mission to "get Yamamoto."

The American P-38 fighter pilots did not encounter Yamamoto's Betty bombers and their escorts by accident. It had indeed been a well-planned ambush. U.S. Naval Intelligence officers had known ahead of time every step that the Japanese naval hero would take on his inspection tour. The only gamble was in the timing of the attack. But this was not really a gamble either, for U.S. Intelligence also knew that Yamamoto was a fanatic about arriving on time. In this instance he had kept a rendezvous with death—virtually to the split second.

How had U.S. Intelligence obtained this vital information? By breaking the Japanese naval code. When Yamamoto's tour and timetable were planned, its details were sent in code by radio to all of the air and naval base commanders whom the admiral planned to visit. Some of Yamamoto's aides thought the information should be delivered by hand by couriers, but they were overruled by top Japanese communications officers who insisted the Japanese code could not be broken. Within hours after the information had been transmitted, however, U.S. Naval Intelligence had not only intercepted it but had also decoded it and given a "plain English text" to the key American commanders, both in Washington and at Henderson Field on Guadalcanal Island in the Pacific. They immediately ordered the mission against Yamamoto.

Solving the War's Most Difficult Riddle

An undeclared, "secret" war began long before actual fighting broke out in World War II. It was a war fought not by great masses of armed men in uniform. It was fought by small groups of men—and often women—sometimes even lone individuals, usually wearing civilian clothes and often unarmed. The general public almost never heard about this secret war fought between the intelligence agents and agencies of rival nations, but it was a real war nonetheless and one that was every bit as important as the armed warfare that was to follow. And even when actual armed conflict began, the secret war between the various intelligence organizations continued—just as it continues today during peacetime.

In Europe in the early 1930s the Germans had developed an electronic cipher machine that enabled them to send secret diplomatic and military messages in what they believed to be unbreakable code. This machine was called "Enigma," meaning a riddle. It was indeed so complicated and sent out such complex messages that for a time it appeared that the Germans were right—they had created a riddle that they alone could solve.

This had been a goal for thousands of years—to create a

form of secret writing that was truly secret. In fact, the word *cryptology*, which is the science of secret writing and its translation or deciphering, comes from two ancient Greek words, *kryptos*, meaning "hidden," and *logos*, meaning "word" or "speech."

As far back as biblical times code was used. In the Old Testament, for example, the word *Shesach* is used to mean "Babel" or "Babylon." Codes were also used by the early Assyrians and Egyptians.

Modern cryptology or cryptography (the words have essentially the same meaning and are used interchangeably) began in Italy during the fifteenth and sixteenth centuries when diplomats began to communicate secretly with each other and with their government. The systems they developed for secret writing, called *enciphering*, are the basis for most of today's codes and ciphers.

In America, methods of secret communication were used by George Washington during the American Revolution. Not only did Washington invent a code with which he and his intelligence agents inside the British lines could communicate, but he also furnished them with an invisible ink called "secret stain," which was made from a formula that modern chemists have been unable to duplicate. A message could be written in secret stain ink between the lines of an innocent letter written in regular ink. The secret stain message would remain invisible until brushed with another liquid, the formula for which was also known only to Washington. Other so-called invisible inks became clearly visible when held over a candle flame, but not so that used by America's revolutionary war leader and first president.

Another United States president, Thomas Jefferson, invented a rotary or wheel cipher machine that was not unlike the German Enigma machine of World War II. Its rotors were turned by hand, of course, and not electronically, but it too produced virtually unbreakable secret messages.

During the American Civil War, both the Union and the Confederacy used rotary machines to encipher and decipher secret messages. Generally, however, more simple methods were used—the substitution of one word for another in a message, or the use of a group of numbers to represent a specific word. The Civil War was the first military conflict in which codes and ciphers were widely used. This was because of the relatively recent invention of the telegraph, which enabled messages to be sent quickly and over a widespread area. During the height of the war, President Abraham Lincoln spent much of his time in the cipher room of the War Department near the White House, where telegraphed messages could be enciphered and deciphered.

During World War I the interception and deciphering of a telegraphed secret message between Germany and Mexico helped the United States decide to enter the war. This was the so-called Zimmermann Telegram. When the war began, German Foreign Secretary Arthur Zimmermann made an attempt to form an alliance between Germany and Mexico. As a part of this bargain, Zimmermann promised that Germany would see to it that Mexico was given the states of New Mexico, Arizona, and Texas if Germany won the war. When this proposal became known to the American public—the message was intercepted and deciphered by the British and given to the United States— many Americans were more than ready for war.

Codes and ciphers were used extensively by America and its allies as well as by Germany and the other Central Powers all during World War I, but between the two world wars the United States fell far behind other countries in developments in cryptography. As a matter of fact, the United States seriously neglected all of its intelligence operations during this period. The American attitude was perhaps best expressed by one United States Secretary of War, Henry L. Stimson, who abolished a key cryptographic

Allan Pinkerton, left, was a Union spy working behind the Confederate lines for President Abraham Lincoln, center, during the American Civil War.

unit with the comment, "Gentlemen do not read other people's mail."

In Europe and the Far East, however, governments and their military organizations continued not only to "read other people's mail" but also to expand and improve upon all of their other intelligence activities. It was out of this effort that the German Enigma machine had grown.

Enigma, which was almost as complicated as one of today's electronic computers, would undoubtedly have remained an unsolvable riddle to Great Britain and its allies in World War II except for one thing: They obtained a key to its operation. And the key was a copy or duplicate of the Enigma machine itself. Stories vary as to exactly how this was accomplished.

According to one story, a Polish mechanic working in a German factory where the Enigma machine was being secretly manufactured kept detailed notes on how the secret cipher machine was made. When the Germans discovered the mechanic's nationality—Germany and Poland were not yet at war, but the two countries were traditional enemies —he was fired and sent back to Poland. There he contacted British officials who smuggled him out of the country and put him to work making a mock-up or copy of the Enigma machine. Another story has it that the Poles actually stole an Enigma machine from the German secret factory and turned it over to the British. A third story was that the Poles themselves built several copies of Enigma and these were turned over to the British, who in turn built an exact duplicate of the German original.

In any event, once British cryptographers had Enigma in their hands they quickly realized what a fiendishly clever device it was. Essentially it was a series of metal drumlike wheels or rotors on the face of which were stamped the letters of the alphabet. Electronically operated, this series of drums could so scramble a single message fed into it by typewriter that, without knowledge of how Enigma worked, a dozen cryptographers might spend a month deciphering that single message. With an actual Enigma machine in their hands, it still took many top British mathematicians with the aid of early computers months to figure out the key to each cipher setting. Once this was accomplished they could do better than read German diplomats' and military officers' mail—they could read every important diplomatic message and military order sent out on the Enigma machine by the top German command. Fortunately, the British accomplished this feat just as World War II began. It was a feat that was to change the entire course of the war. Without its accomplishment the Allies could well have lost the conflict. It was also a feat that was kept virtually secret until the mid-1970s, more than a quarter of a century after Allied victory over the Axis powers, Germany, Italy, and Japan.

Adolf Hitler had courted Japan as an ally long before World War II began. To win Japan's favor, Hitler personally ordered that the first simple version of Enigma be given to the Japanese in the early 1930s. The Japanese made certain modifications in it and used it mainly for diplomatic messages. Later, the more complicated German Enigma machine was also shared with Japan and was used by all of the Japanese military forces throughout the war. In similar fashion, when the Enigma riddle was solved Great Britain and the United States shared this information.

When World War II began, there was naturally an increased interest in cryptography on the part of the American diplomatic and military services. Before the United States entered the war, U.S. Intelligence and its operation called "Magic" had broken the Japanese diplomatic or so-called Purple code, which was transmitted via the early simple version of the Enigma machine. Magic was shared with Great Britain. Great Britain's solution for the riddle of the far more complex Enigma for sending both military and diplomatic messages was called "Ultra Secret" or simply "Ultra." Ultra was shared with the United States. It was the sharing of this latter secret that almost resulted in letting both the Germans and the Japanese know that the Enigma riddle had been solved. If this had happened, the Axis powers would have immediately switched to some other code or cipher method and the Allies would have had to start all over again in solving it.

As soon as the Enigma riddle had been solved, the major Allied problem had become one of who was to be given the military information resulting from the interception and deciphering of the enemy's Enigma messages. If the Germans or Japanese sent out messages to their military forces to make an attack on the Allies at a certain time and place, should the Allied military commanders be given this information? The immediate answer would seem to be yes. But if the Allies seemed to know every time and place that the Axis powers were to attack, then the Axis leaders would soon begin to suspect that their code had been broken. The answer, therefore, seemed to be that information from Enigma intercepts should only be given to certain top commanders at certain times and it should only be acted upon if a convincing "cover" story could be used to fool the enemy into thinking that the Allies had received their advance information not by breaking the Enigma code but by some other means—perhaps from spies, or agents as they were usually called, who were also key sources of information.

This called for some hard decisions on the part of Allied leaders. Early in the war, for example, British Prime Minister Winston Churchill was given forewarning by his intelligence staff that the German *Luftwaffe* was about to bomb the English cathedral city of Coventry. Churchill could have ordered all civilians to leave the city, but word of such a move before the city was actually bombed would almost certainly have reached the Germans, arousing their

suspicions about how the British had obtained foreknowl-
edge of the raid. In the end, Churchill remained silent,
hundreds of Coventry civilians became casualties, but
British knowledge of Germany's Enigma remained an Ultra Secret.

When the United States entered the war, Ultra was the
key to vital American actions in the Pacific. Perhaps its most
important early role was in the Battle of Midway Island in
the spring of 1942. Japanese naval messages intercepted by
Ultra forewarned U.S. Admiral Chester Nimitz of the
forthcoming attack on Midway. They also indicated that
the Japanese would attack the Aleutian Islands in order
to draw the American fleet away from Midway to the
north. Thus forewarned, Nimitz refused to allow the
American war fleet to be feinted away from Midway. In
the naval battle itself U.S. dive bombers sank several Japanese aircraft carriers, a blow from which Japan never
recovered.

Regarding this turning point of the naval war in the Pacific, Admiral Nimitz later said, "Had we lacked early information of the Japanese movements and intentions, the
Battle of Midway would have ended differently."

Unfortunately, a newspaper correspondent, Stanley
Johnston of the Chicago *Tribune,* reported the fact that the
Japanese naval code had been broken and that the U.S.
Navy knew all about the plans for the attack on Midway
several weeks before it took place. Prime Minister Churchill personally protested this breach of security to President Franklin Roosevelt.

The United States tightened security measures to prevent jeopardizing the Ultra Secret it shared with Great
Britain, and no further breaches occurred in the Pacific
until the spring of 1943. This was when Admiral Yamamoto was shot down. It was Ultra that had revealed where
Yamamoto was going on his inspection tour and exactly
when he would be there. The breach of security involved

the fact that the United States had no cover story to indicate how its forces had learned Yamamoto's timetable unless
it was by breaking the Japanese code. But the Japanese at
first stubbornly refused to come to this conclusion, putting
down Yamamoto's death—which proved to be an enormous blow to Japanese morale—as one of the accidental
misfortunes of war.

Gradually, however, the Japanese realized their code
must have been broken both before the Battle of Midway
and before Yamamoto was shot down, and they changed it.
This happened at least two other times during the war,
once when American agents broke into the office of the
Japanese military attaché in Lisbon, Portugal, and com-
promised the Japanese code and again after secret military information was published in a popular American
magazine, *Colliers*. Again the Japanese changed their code
and U.S. cryptologists had to begin their decoding efforts
all over again. Fortunately, these efforts were successful.

Codes and Ciphers in World War II

While the electronic machines for enciphering and deciphering messages in World War II reached a point of near perfection, the principles on which the codes and ciphers themselves were based were hundreds of years old.

The words *codes* and *ciphers* are often used interchangeably as if they mean the same thing. Actually, there is a difference between them. Ciphers usually involve the use of single letters of the alphabet. Sometimes they use two letters, and only rarely three. Codes involve the use of parts of words, whole words, and sometimes phrases or entire sentences.

Despite their apparent complexity, there are only two ways to create codes and ciphers—transposition and substitution. This has remained true since the first secret message was written. In transposition ciphers the letters in a word are shifted from one place to another. Thus the letters in the word ATTACK might be simply reversed and become KCATTA. In substitution ciphers the letters in the original word or sentence (called *plaintext*) are exchanged for different letters, symbols, or even numbers to create a *ciphertext*. Thus ATTACK might become a jumble of letters, BUUBDL.

Obviously, both the sender and the receiver of such messages must know whether transposition or substitution is being used—sometimes it is both—and exactly how. This is called the *key*. For example, the substitution cipher of BUUBDL was arrived at simply by substituting the letter *B* for the letter *A*, *U* for the letter *T*, *D* for *C*, and *L* for *K* in the word ATTACK. This is *also* a form of transposition cipher since the substitute letters were selected by simply moving one letter to the right in each letter of the alphabet that was used in the original word, ATTACK. The letter *A* became *B*, *T* became *U*, *C* became *D*, and *K* became *L*. An experienced *cryptanalyst*—one who deciphers a ciphertext—would solve this enciphered message at a glance.

In actual practice, of course, few single-word messages or *cryptograms* would be sent. Instead they would be sent in phrases, sentences, and complete paragraphs. A typical cryptogram might be: ATTACK AT ZERO SIX HUNDRED HOURS FRIDAY. But once this message was enciphered it would not be sent in word groups of differing lengths. It would probably be broken up into five-letter groups, which in this case would leave two blank spaces after the final grouping:

ATTAC

KATZE

ROSIX

HUNDR

EDHOU

RSFRI

DAYQQ

These blank spaces would be filled in with extra random letters called *nulls*. In this case the letter *Q* is a null. The above message is only broken up into five-letter word groups; it is not enciphered. To encipher this plaintext,

Using a homemade cipher disk, this young man is deciphering a message. This is a substitution cipher. The incomplete signature represented by the numbers 11.23.10.9 will be "Fred."

transposition or substitution or both would be used to scramble the message completely.

In all of the above examples just one alphabet is used. Because this method dates back so far in history it is usually referred to as the Julius Caesar system. In modern cryptography systems such as those used in World War II, two or more cipher alphabets are usually used to encipher even a single message. This was largely made possible by the development of such electronic machines as Enigma. Each of the multiple rotors or wheels on Enigma bore a separate alphabet. Thus, depending upon the number of rotors used, up to several hundred thousand single alphabet letter substitutions could be made at one setting of the machine. Each time the machine was reset, another several hundred thousand variations would result. When the British solved the Enigma riddle via the use of computers, they learned what letters in each of these alphabets would be used as a result of each key setting and were able to unscramble even the most astronomically scrambled message.

In addition to codes and ciphers there are methods of secret writing called *concealment systems*. Besides writing with invisible ink, these may include hiding a secret message within an apparently innocent communication. If only the first letters of the phrase SHELTER OUR STRAWBERRIES are used, the message becomes SOS, the international distress call for help. Incidentally, the usual method for transmitting SOS via the so-called Morse code, which is represented by ... --- ..., is actually a form of substitution cipher.

Concealment systems were used only to a limited degree in World War II. Next to the breaking of codes and ciphers, the most important means of obtaining secret information about enemy activity was through the use of agents.

Spies Inside the United States

It was not only Great Britain and the United States that were successful in breaking the enemies' codes and deciphering their ciphers before and during World War II. Germany and Japan also had a major degree of success in breaking the Allies' codes, especially the American Gray code used for diplomatic messages, which was created by a system called "Superencipherment." Superencipherment was intended to make messages doubly secure, but because of certain flaws it made decipherment doubly easy. Unfortunately, the United States did not realize this for almost a year after Pearl Harbor. When it did the Gray code was discarded and a new one called M-138 was substituted. This code plus others developed by U.S. Naval Intelligence remained unbreakable throughout the war. Great Britain reacted much more quickly at the mere suggestion that any of its codes had been broken and immediately substituted new ones. In addition, both the United States and Britain soon developed their own cipher machines that were every bit as efficient as Enigma, and the Germans and Japanese never succeeded in obtaining duplicates of these.

Germany's greatest success in obtaining secret information from the Allies, especially the United States, was through the use of spies.

The German secret service (called "Abwehr") was headed by Admiral Wilhelm Canaris. A veteran of Germany's naval warfare in World War I, Canaris had remained in the navy between wars and had become interested in intelligence work even before Hitler came to power in 1933. Under Hitler, Canaris was put in charge of all of the Nazi intelligence activities, many of which included the secret rearmament of Germany, which had been forbidden to rearm under the Versailles Treaty that ended World War I. An unassuming, wrinkle-faced little man, Canaris did not look in the least like one of the world's top spymasters. But that was exactly what he was.

The Abwehr was divided into three sections. Section I collected intelligence information about other nations' military organizations. Section II conducted sabotage operations against Germany's enemies. Section III was engaged mainly in counterintelligence work, that is, catching any foreign agents working inside Germany. It was Section I that conducted espionage operations inside the United States and Great Britain.

In the early 1930s one of the U.S. Army Air Force's most carefully guarded military secrets was the Norden bombsight. This precision bombsight was developed by an American engineer, Carl L. Norden, and a U.S. Navy officer, Captain Frederick I. Entwhistle. It enabled a bombardier to release a plane's bombs at exactly the right moment and hit a pinpoint target—"put a bomb in a picklebarrel," as air force flyers said.

Although the way the bombsight worked remained a secret, most nations of the world knew that the United States had such a device. In fact, Japan tried unsuccessfully to buy one in 1932, and Great Britain was not successful in obtaining one until 1940. But Germany, under Canaris and his Abwehr agents, obtained detailed drawings of the bombsight as early as 1937!

The Norden bombsight drawings were obtained by a man named Herman Lang, a draftsman and inspector in the Norden bombsight factory in New York City. Born in Germany, Lang had been a naturalized U.S. citizen for a dozen years, but he was still loyal to Germany. He was typical of the kind of person the Germans recruited as agents. While he was not active in pro-Nazi meetings or demonstrations in the United States, he did have many German-American friends. One of these friends was a man named Henry Sohn, who was already working for the Abwehr.

When Sohn learned that Lang was working in the Norden plant, he encouraged Lang to make copies of all of the drawings that were available to him. This Lang did, taking them home with him at night and on weekends and laboriously tracing copies of them by hand. (Such lack of security was not uncommon before the United States entered the war; after Pearl Harbor security measures were greatly strengthened.)

Once the drawings were traced, Sohn contacted the Abwehr in Germany and told them to send a special courier to pick them up. The courier was another German-born naturalized American citizen especially chosen by Canaris for the job—a former American textile manufacturer named Nicholas Ritter. Ritter's American business had gone into bankruptcy during the Depression of the 1930s, and he had returned to Germany and rejoined the army, in which he had been an officer during World War I. Because Ritter had spent ten years in the United States and spoke English fluently, he was assigned to Abwehr. When Sohn's message arrived requesting a special courier, Canaris decided that Ritter would be ideal for the job.

Ritter returned to the United States disguised as a businessman seeking manufacturing contracts. He immediately contacted Sohn who in turn contacted Lang who turned over his bombsight drawings to Ritter in exchange for fifteen hundred dollars. Ritter smuggled the drawings out of the country rolled up inside an umbrella, and within a matter of weeks German engineers had used them to build a bombsight that was every bit as good as if not better than the original Norden device.

But before he left the United States, Ritter also made other contacts with prospective Abwehr agents. One of these men, Everett M. Roeder, worked in the Sperry gyroscope plant on Long Island, which manufactured special electronic equipment for the U.S. military forces. Roeder later furnished the Abwehr with drawings of the radio system for new air force bombers as well as blueprints of an aerial range finder, instruments that would enable a pilot to fly blind in fog, a bank-and-turn indicator, and a highly specialized navigational compass.

Other contacts made by Ritter included Frederick J. Duquesne, a native South African who worked for the Germans because he hated the British after his mother was killed years earlier in the Boer War. Duquesne and agents he in turn recruited succeeded in turning over to the Abwehr a number of other secret devices. These included blueprints for a powerful, long-life storage battery, and a catapult and arresting gear for launching and retrieving carrier-based aircraft.

All in all, at the time World War II began in Europe the German Abwehr had literally dozens of agents working in the United States. Once Hitler ordered his armies into Poland, however, on September 1, 1939, the Abwehr was forced to concentrate its main efforts on intelligence work in European countries, and especially Great Britain. It would not renew its great interest in the United States until the Japanese attacked Pearl Harbor on December 7, 1941, bringing America into the war.

Spies in Great Britain

Hitler never believed that Great Britain would declare war on Germany. He was convinced that if the British were not too badly provoked they would find some way to keep out of any conflicts on the Continent. He had good reason for thinking so. Like the United States, Britain had become increasingly isolationist after World War I, wanting nothing to do with foreign wars. This attitude was best expressed by British Prime Minister Neville Chamberlain who made every effort to appease Hitler in his bold moves to take over territory outside of Germany's borders. In addition, there was a certain amount of pro-Nazi and pro-Fascist feeling in Britain especially among some members of the upper class. One English aristocrat, in fact, headed a popular organization known as Sir Oswald Mosley's British Union of Fascists.

Hitler's hope was that Britain would continue to appease Germany as it rolled over Europe. Then, with this conquest completed, Germany and Britain with its vast colonial empire could rule the world together, or—if the British objected to this arrangement—Hitler could conquer Great Britain at his leisure.

One of the points about which Hitler was badly mistaken in his assessment of the British was in assuming that because some of them seemed to be pro-Nazi or pro-Fascist they would actually fight on the German or Italian side against Great Britain. Even Sir Oswald Mosley made it clear that his followers should do nothing to harm Great Britain in the event of war. Actually, when war did come, Mosley's organization, like similar radical isolationist and anti-Semitic groups in the United States, simply vanished in the face of patriotic unity against the Axis powers.

Because of the natural loyalty of almost all of the British, the few German agents who did get into the British Isles had great difficulty in recruiting other spies or even in carrying on much successful espionage activity themselves. One agent, however, did manage to score at least one major success. This was in locating and identifying British radar towers and forwarding this information to the German *Luftwaffe* who used it with marked effect in the aerial Battle of Britain.

Radar had been patented by Britain's Robert Watson-Watt in 1935. The Germans had heard about radar for some time, but they did not know how much the British had developed it or whether they had actually installed it anywhere. Radar, German scientists knew, would make it possible for the British to detect approaching *Luftwaffe* aircraft long before they could be heard or seen. A device that used the special *ultrashort* or *micro* properties of electromagnetic waves, *radar* was coined from the first letters of the words "radio detecting and ranging." Its perfection by the British would give them a tremendous advantage in any air war between the Royal Air Force and the *Luftwaffe*.

By 1938 Canaris had more than 250 German agents in the British Isles. Although few of them met with any marked success in recruiting additional agents in Britain, several of them were able on their own to send back to Germany detailed maps of British airfields, locations of

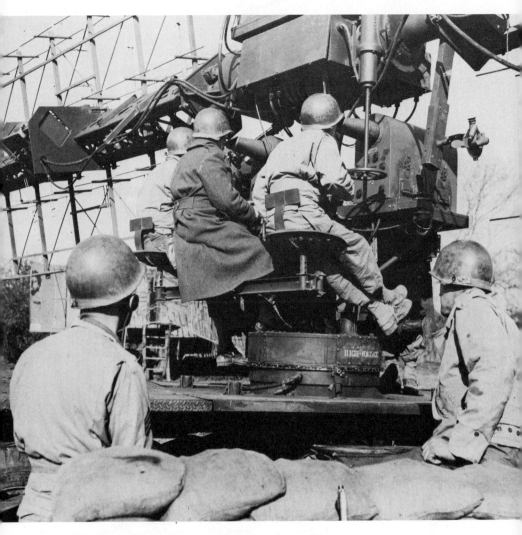

*These U.S. Army men are operating an early
and somewhat primitive radarscope.*

factories, ports, docks, warehouses, and other key points that were later used as targets by the *Luftwaffe* bombers in the air *blitzkrieg* (lightning war) of 1940–41. Gradually, however, British counterintelligence, which was called MI-5 (Military Intelligence, section 5), tracked down most of these spies one at a time and they were shot, imprisoned, or allowed to return to Germany to spy on the Germans for the British. These last were called "double agents." Some double agents were allowed to remain in Britain and send back a limited amount of information to Germany, but this was done under the watchful eye of MI-5. Sir John Masterman, who took part in this intelligence activity for the British all during World War II, later stated that *all* German spies in Britain were caught and used or "run" as double agents, but this is doubtful. Masterman's "Double Cross System," as it was labeled, was, however, enormously successful in defeating Canaris's espionage efforts.

One German spy, whom the British did not catch until he had done a considerable amount of damage to the Allied cause, was Arthur G. Owens, whose code name was Snow.

Owens or Snow was a so-called mole or sleeper agent. This was an agent who was sent into the enemy's country long before war began and then allowed to remain quietly there without contacting home base until fighting actually began. Then the agent was alerted and was expected to start sending back information about current military activities. Some moles or sleepers remained hidden quietly for months and even years before they were called into action. Some were never caught.

For example, a mole similar to Owens, although a far more damaging one, was Harold "Kim" Philby, a brilliant Russian agent who penetrated Britain's topmost Secret Intelligence Service (SIS) during World War II and, before he was discovered as a Russian spy, came close to becoming its chief after the war. He escaped to the Soviet Union in 1962.

Owens was one of the few citizens of the British Isles whom Canaris was able to recruit as an Abwehr spy. A Welshman by birth, Owens had lived in England since 1933, but he was still a strong Welsh nationalist who greatly disliked the English. In England he had become a traveling salesman for an electronics company. His salesman's job frequently took him to the Continent, and he usually returned with a considerable amount of information about recent developments and inventions at the electronics firms he visited. Before long the British Secret Intelligence Service persuaded Owens to give this information to SIS.

Shortly afterward Owens was also contacted by an Abwehr agent at a German social club in London to which Owens belonged. Without much persuasion Owens decided also to go to work for the Germans. Still disliking the British and wanting a fully independent Wales, Owens secretly hoped that Germany would win the war. His German contact sympathized with him in these feelings, or pretended to do so, and offered to pay him considerably more than the British were paying him for his espionage services. Owens accepted. Thus he indeed became a double agent, but a double agent loyal to Germany and not Great Britain.

On a visit to Hamburg, Germany, Owens met and was greatly impressed by a man called "Dr. Hubert Rantzau." Actually, Dr. Rantzau was none other than Nicholas Ritter, who had done such excellent work in the United States in obtaining and smuggling out the Norden bombsight drawings. It was Ritter who now instructed Owens to return to England and become a sleeper until war broke out, which in fact would happen within a few months.

When World War II began, Owens was alerted by a certain song played on a Hamburg radio station that could be heard in England. He immediately went to work sending via shortwave radio information vital to the *Luftwaffe*—current weather reports, ceiling and visibility, and weather forecasts for all areas the Germans might want to bomb. He also managed to obtain and send details about specific airfields where the RAF was currently located, the strength of RAF units, and other valuable information.

But it was in mid-September 1939 that Owens sent his most dramatic message: The British had not only perfected radar but there were radar installations already in operation all along the British coast from the Isle of Wight to the Orkney Islands. This was a wall of detection devices that the *Luftwaffe* could not possibly avoid in any raids on the British Isles.

Curiously, *Luftwaffe* reconnaissance planes had already photographed these towers, but photo interpreters in the Third Reich had decided they were ordinary radio towers.

Canaris immediately described Owens's report as "one of the most important pieces of intelligence we'll ever get."

The *Luftwaffe* immediately went to work destroying these newly discovered radar towers by bombing them. If they had completely destroyed them, Great Britain might well have lost the early air war. And if this air war had been lost, Britain would undoubtedly have been invaded because the *Luftwaffe* attacks were meant to be the opening phase of Hitler's invasion campaign called "Operation Sea Lion." But Hermann Goering, chief of the *Luftwaffe,* regarded attacks on the radar towers as a waste of time. He was determined to destroy all of the Spitfire and Hurricane fighter planes of the RAF Fighter Command and anything else simply interfered with this plan.

In the middle of August 1940, Goering told his flyers, "Until further orders operations are to be directed exclusively against the enemy air force. Other targets should be ignored. It is doubtful," Goering continued, "whether there is any point in continuing the attacks on radar sites since none of these has so far been put out of operation."

Goering, of course, was dead wrong, since half-a-dozen radar sites had been put out of commission. Nevertheless, only two more attacks were made against them—one of the key reasons why the RAF won the Battle of Britain and earned from Prime Minister Winston Churchill, who succeeded Chamberlain and did away with appeasement, the undying words of praise: "Never in the field of human conflict was so much owed by so many to so few."

Arthur Owens, or Snow, was arrested by MI-5 in the spring of 1941 while sending out a weather report to Germany via shortwave radio. He was imprisoned but not executed mainly because the British were not *positive* he was indeed a double agent who was mainly loyal to Germany. In fact, there were those who said he was actually a *triple* agent—a spy who pretended to be loyal to the British who also pretended to be loyal to the Germans but was really loyal to the British! In any event, Owens was released from prison and melted into the mysterious mists from whence so many spies have seemed to come.

VI

Intelligence Comrades-in-Arms

Until the 1970s, more than a quarter of a century after World War II had ended, only a handful of people knew that during much of the war the real headquarters of the British Secret Intelligence Service was actually in the United States.

This intelligence headquarters was called the British Security Coordination, or simply BSC, to hide its true identity from the American people as well as from any prying enemy agents. President Franklin Roosevelt knew of its existence, of course, since it had been established in the United States as a part of his close collaboration with Prime Minister Winston Churchill. J. Edgar Hoover and certain members of his Federal Bureau of Investigation also knew about the BSC, but few other people did.

The BSC was established in New York City in 1940 many months before the United States entered the war. It was headed by Great Britain's top intelligence expert, Sir William Stephenson, to whom Churchill had given the code name Intrepid.

A Canadian by birth, Stephenson had fought in the trenches in Europe for two years during World War I before joining the British Royal Flying Corps. Several of

Britain's Sir William Stephenson,
whose code name, "Intrepid," was given to him
by Prime Minister Winston Churchill.

Stephenson's detailed combat reports about German avi-
ation came to the attention of Sir Reginald Hall, the British
Intelligence officer who had intercepted and deciphered
the famous Zimmermann Telegram that had helped
prompt the United States to enter the war. Hall was always
on the lookout for able men to add to his staff and Stephenson seemed an ideal candidate.

Stephenson was by this time an air ace with twenty-six
victories to his credit. One of the German flyers he had shot
down was Lothar von Richthofen, brother of the famous
Red Baron, Manfred von Richthofen. Later Stephenson
himself was shot down and taken prisoner. He escaped,
however, and when he returned to the British lines he
wrote another detailed report, this time about German
prisoner-of-war camps. This report also came to Hall's attention and this time Hall requested that Stephenson be
transferred to Hall's intelligence staff.

After World War I Stephenson returned to Canada, but
Hall soon persuaded him to come to London and rejoin
the British Secret Intelligence Service. Before long he became Winston Churchill's personal intelligence chief.
When Churchill became Britain's prime minister on May
10, 1940, Stephenson was named head of SIS. A few months
later it looked like Germany was about to invade Britain.
If so, it was likely the British Isles would be conquered.
In this event Churchill planned to fight on from some
overseas base, hopefully in the United States. To pave
the way for such an eventuality Churchill and Roosevelt
decided that Britain's Intelligence headquarters should
be transferred to New York City under a disguised name.
Thus BSC was born.

The major problem was that the United States was still
a neutral nation. President Roosevelt solved this problem
simply by pretending to be neutral while secretly seeing to
it that the United States aided Great Britain. Roosevelt's

efforts, if they had been disclosed at the time, might well have led to his impeachment, since there were many congressmen who were violently opposed to America's entry into the war. Roosevelt himself recognized and privately acknowledged the possibility of his being impeached, but this did not change his firm belief that Hitler and his followers represented an evil that had to be eliminated from the world no matter what the cost.

The role of BSC, as Roosevelt and Churchill saw it, was to work with the United States in establishing a worldwide intelligence network that would help in attacking and defeating the Axis powers. But at this time the United States had virtually no intelligence service like that of the British. It had the FBI, of course, but that agency was meant to protect the internal security of the nation. It was not intended as an agency that would engage in worldwide intelligence activity—guerrilla warfare, sabotage, espionage, and the interception and deciphering of other nations' secret communications. The U.S. military services, it was true, had their intelligence sections, but these did not entirely meet the need either, and they were not apt to go into high gear unless the nation actually entered the war. Roosevelt knew that a special new intelligence agency must be created, the first of its kind in American history. The man he chose for the job was William "Wild Bill" Donovan.

Donovan's background and experience were not unlike those of Stephenson with whom he was soon to become a comrade-in-arms. A veteran of World War I in which his bravery had won him his nickname as well as several of this nation's and France's top awards for courage, Donovan had fought in France with the famous Rainbow Division, which was made up of National Guard units from all over the United States. The National Guard unit in which Donovan had served as a major and later a colonel was

Major General William "Wild Bill" Donovan,
head of the United States Office of Strategic Services (OSS).
Donovan and Stephenson worked closely together to establish
a worldwide intelligence network.

New York's famous "Fighting 69th." Another member of
the Fighting 69th had been the poet Joyce Kilmer. In fact,
Sergeant Kilmer, author of the poem "Trees," was with
Donovan on a scouting patrol mission along the Ourcq
River in July 1918 on the day he was killed. Another
famous member of the Rainbow Division was Douglas
MacArthur, then a colonel, who would become one of
the great heroes of World War II in the Pacific War.

After World War I, Donovan returned to civilian life
to practice law, but he kept up an interest in the military,
especially those aspects of the military that had to do with
making intelligence estimates of foreign powers' preparations for war. He made several fact-finding trips to Europe,
concentrating on Russia and Germany, and reported his
findings to the U.S. State Department. His reports on Germany's preparations for World War II should have alerted
the State Department, but America was at the height of its
"America First," isolationist period and talk of war was
ignored because it was unpopular. Donovan did, however,
share his findings with several British Intelligence observers, and this brought him to the attention of both
Churchill and Stephenson.

When World War II began in Europe, Roosevelt and
Churchill started a secret correspondence. This correspondence was begun by Roosevelt in 1939 even before Churchill became prime minister in place of Neville Chamberlain. Churchill was then First Lord of the Admiralty but had
his finger on most of Britain's intelligence efforts. Roosevelt
explained that he needed to know exactly how successfully
or unsuccessfully Britain's war effort was going if he wanted
to be able to convince the American people that the United
States should join the war on Britain's side. Churchill was
only too eager to oblige since he knew Britain must have
U.S. aid if it were to win the war. When Churchill became
prime minister, his detailed accounts of the war's progress

were sent firsthand to Roosevelt via Stephenson or one of Stephenson's trusted aides.

Very early in the war Donovan began to play the same role with Roosevelt as Stephenson played with Churchill—that of personal intelligence chief. But when Roosevelt asked Donovan to establish a new U.S. Intelligence service like that of the British, Donovan at first declined. He did not like the idea of becoming a desk-bound general—or, as he called it, a "chair-borne commando"—rather than lead a division in battle. But Roosevelt was persuasive regarding the desperate need for such an agency and Donovan finally agreed to accept the post.

To confuse American isolationists regarding its purpose, the new agency was called the Office of the Coordinator of Information (COI). Donovan was named its director in 1941. The COI kept its title until the following year when, with the United States having gone to war, its existence if not its activities could be openly recognized. In 1942 it became the Office of Strategic Services (OSS) and Donovan was named its commanding major general. From this point on Donovan and Stephenson and their unified organizations worked as an inseparable Allied Intelligence team to defeat the Axis powers.

Donovan had no historical American guidelines to follow in creating the OSS. The only vaguely similar organization in United States history had been the nation's first official Secret Service established by Allan Pinkerton during the Civil War. The owner of a Chicago detective agency, Pinkerton had been hired by President Abraham Lincoln to travel inside the Confederate lines and report his findings to Lincoln and Union General George B. McClellan. Pinkerton, disguised as Mr. E. J. Allen, a Southern gentleman from Augusta, Georgia, had been a courageous but inefficient spy. He furnished the Union with as much misinformation as he did factual information, and Donovan was familiar enough with American history to know that

Lincoln and the Union cause would probably have been better off without Pinkerton's Secret Service efforts. Donovan was determined his organization would serve President Roosevelt and the American war effort in far better fashion. In this he succeeded.

How British and American Agents Were Trained

Both the British and the Americans had intelligence training camps in North America. The British one was in Canada on the northern shore of Lake Ontario near the United States border. The American one was in Fairfax, Virginia, near Washington, D.C. Britain's so-called Camp X was established in Canada in 1940 to avoid the legal problems of training and using American citizens as combatants while the United States was still a neutral nation. The Washington OSS Station S grew out of Donovan's early prewar experiments in using civilian rather than military personnel to do intelligence work.

Despite Donovan's all-out efforts to gain cooperation from the U.S. military, both the army and navy fought against what they regarded as civilian OSS intrusion into military affairs during most of the war. J. Edgar Hoover and his FBI were also far from cooperative, mainly because Hoover was jealous of Donovan and fearful that the OSS might become more important than the FBI. As a result, even after Pearl Harbor Donovan found he had enemies to fight both at home and overseas. But President Roosevelt had chosen the right man. Donovan was as heroic in the bureaucratic wars as he had been in combat in

World War I and eventually his stubborn determination to create an American Intelligence service from scratch was a key factor in winning the war.

While the training and activities of the behind-the-lines agents were by far the most romantic and glamorous aspects of the BSC and the OSS, such cloak-and-dagger work was by no means their only important role. Some observers thought that an even more important role was played by the people in Research and Analysis (R&A), most of whom worked in BSC headquarters in New York and OSS headquarters in Washington.

R&A personnel were drawn from the ranks of students and scholars throughout the world. It was important that they could both read and speak fluently at least one language besides English. This was so they could translate foreign newspapers, technical journals, business reports and similar material and thus piece together a true picture of an enemy nation's economy and its military activities.

Foreign publications were either bought in neutral countries or smuggled out of enemy or enemy-occupied countries by agents. The information they provided was invaluable. A local German newspaper might report the names of certain infantry officers who attended a dance and thus disclose the location of a Nazi division. A study of European farm publications might disclose food shortages or a lack of them. Obituary columns often indicated the loss of key enemy leaders.

When the war began, terrain maps of enemy countries were in great demand and not too many were available. Eventually this problem was solved by aerial photo reconnaissance missions that provided detailed photographic maps of entire nations. Before then, however, R&A duplicated maps from back issues of travel and educational magazines as well as textbooks. R&A also provided original maps drawn with the aid of people who were natives of certain foreign regions. Transportation maps were also vital, especially prior to an invasion. Through careful research R&A determined not only the highway and railway network of an enemy country but also what state of repair or disrepair it was in as a result of aerial bombardment.

As the military began to be provided with such valuable and often life-saving information, it began to have at least a grudging respect for the work of Donovan's and Stephenson's Research and Analysis departments.

But while the work of R&A was difficult and demanding, it was not essentially dangerous. The dangerous work was done by the cloak-and-dagger agents for whom a single mistake meant death. To avoid making such mistakes, trainees were put through some of the most difficult training imaginable.

Because the United States was a melting pot of nationalities filled with people of mixed racial backgrounds, it was an ideal place to recruit prospective behind-the-lines agents. Many recruits were well-known personalities. Among these were former Notre Dame and professional football star Joe Savoldi, circus owner John Ringling North, motion-picture star Sterling Hayden, former President Theodore Roosevelt's grandson Quentin Roosevelt, Hobart College President Willaim A. Eddy, and numerous others. Some were less well known but had unique and badly needed qualifications. Among these were Hollywood stuntmen, former European waiters and bartenders, former members of foreign military services, and even a team of European mountain climbers as well as several religious missionaries.

Canada also provided well-known cloak-and-dagger candidates, the most famous of whom was the future Canadian Prime Minister Lester B. Pearson. Others included ship captains with special knowledge of foreign ports, members of the Royal Canadian Mounted Police, and former foreign professors who had fled from Europe in the face of Hitler's Jewish purges. British playwright and actor Noel Coward was enlisted to report on conversations he had or overheard while on concert tour of South America where Nazi sympathizers were numerous.

Both the BSC and the OSS always had members who acted as talent scouts who kept an eye out for needed recruits. When they were spotted, they were given a background security check even before they were asked if they were interested in intelligence work. If they passed the security check and their answer was yes, they were sent to an assessment school where their physical stamina and mental stability were severely tested. Behind-the-lines work was both lonely and demanding and a candidate had to be in top shape both mentally and physically to keep from cracking up under the stress of active espionage work when he or she went into the field.

Station S in Virginia was disguised as an Army Rehabilitation Camp for mental patients. Here OSS candidates discarded not only their civilian clothes but also their civilian identities. They were told to pick a new name and make up an autobiographical background or "cover" story about themselves. They would be expected to stick to their new false identity no matter what situation they found themselves in. All during their training, regular OSS members would try to trap candidates into innocent conversations in which they might disclose their true identities and thus break their cover.

The training day at Station S was from dawn until well after dark. Calisthenics, running obstacle courses, and similar strenuous activities were part of the physical conditioning course. Mental conditioning included such exercises as deciding exactly who the person was who had moved out of a room and left behind numerous articles of clothing, newspapers, timetables, and the like. Candidates were expected to reason out the missing person's age, weight, hair shade, nationality, and occupation just from the articles left in the room.

A test for reaction to stress might be trying to build a bridge across a stream with only the natural materials at hand while supposedly being "helped" by several other candidates. Actually the helper candidates would be regular OSS staff members who did everything conceivable to prevent the bridge's being built.

There were also so-called Stress Interviews in which candidates would be given third-degree grilling by staff members acting as enemy interrogation police. Alone in a darkened room and seated in a straight-backed chair with a powerful light shining in his or her face, a candidate would be questioned mercilessly for hour after hour about his or her activities in the past few weeks, accused of all manner of crimes, threatened with physical punishment, and then—no matter what the candidate's reaction—told the test had been failed. This last statement was often the most important part of the Stress Interview, because OSS senior members watched closely for the candidate's reaction to apparent failure. If he or she then broke down emotionally, the candidate was released from the course. This was harsh treatment, but inability to stand up under the most severe kind of interrogation could be fatal in the event an agent was captured behind the lines.

Those candidates who successfully passed the OSS assessment tests were assigned to advanced training classes. Here the murderous techniques of disabling or killing an enemy quietly and efficiently were taught. These included not only such so-called martial arts as karate and jujitsu or judo, but also the skilled use of knives for silent assassination. These were the same techniques that were taught to special American and British combat battalions such as the Rangers and Commandos and usually an experienced Ranger or Commando acted as an instructor in the training of agents.

The use and maintenance of most small firearms were also taught as well as how to use and repair cameras and shortwave radios. Each prospective agent also had to study codes and ciphers and each was given his own code name and was required to memorize certain ciphers for behind-the-lines use. Certain agents were also taught the use of high explosives for use in destroying trains, bridges, and even ships in port. Plastic explosives were perfected in World War II. These were adhesive, puttylike substances that could be attached to a metal surface simply by slapping them firmly against that surface. Detonators were also attached so that the plastic bomb could be exploded at the desired time when the agent had left the scene.

After they were trained many American agents were often sent out on actual missions within the United States. In cooperation with the FBI, whose own agents were forewarned of the exercise, agents were assigned the job of secretly breaking into a certain office or factory and stealing or photographing classified documents. So successful were some of these operations that Donovan was able to get the FBI to tell certain office managers that their security measures were inadequate and showed them microfilmed copies of their top secret documents to prove it.

The final phase of an agent's training was parachute school. For American agents who were going to be dropped into occupied Europe, parachute school was usually held in Britain. After this, agents were told where they were going to be dropped and then they memorized maps of the area in which they would work. They were then dressed in civilian clothing suited to the role they would play and given all of the required papers, documents, and other personal items they would be expected to carry—identification cards, ration cards, money, cigarettes or tobacco, and perhaps even correspondence—a letter from a mother or sweetheart, for example.

Equipping spies with authentic clothing and other ma-

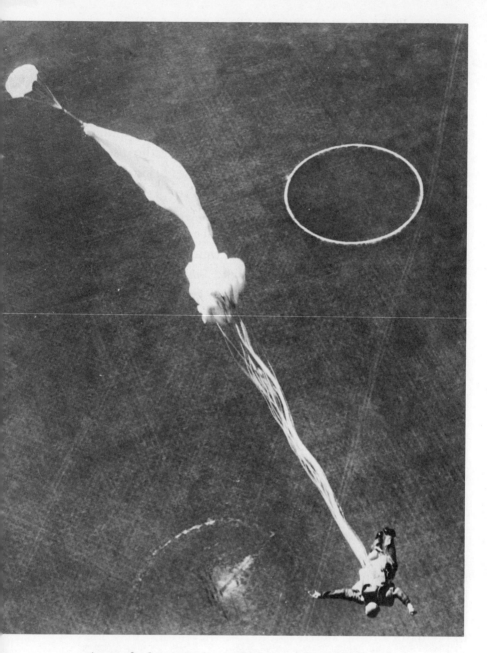

Agents had to practice making parachute landings within a specific area before they were dropped behind enemy lines.

terial was one of the most painstaking and difficult tasks of both the BSC and the OSS. Both in Toronto and New York immigrants who had escaped from Nazi-controlled Europe were given new clothing, new pens, pencils, and other personal items in exchange for their old possessions that were needed by agents. Sometimes clothing was stolen from laundries and dry cleaners and the laundry marks carefully removed. People who lost clothing in this way were always paid for their losses with money given the laundries or dry cleaners by the government. Secondhand stores and pawnshops were also carefully combed for authentic European clothing, jewelry, and other items. Cloth was also smuggled out of Europe to manufacture clothing. When this was done, infinite pains had to be taken to make sure that European methods of manufacture were used. For example, buttons were sewn on with parallel stitching rather than crisscross as they were in the United States and Canada, and suit coats or jackets were fully lined European-style rather than half or yoke lined. Stockings were usually hand-knitted, and shoes were often handmade and then worn until they no longer looked new. Money, in small denominations, was either smuggled out of Europe or counterfeited. If the money given agents was counterfeit, it had to be artificially aged because an agent disguised as a French peasant, for example, would be immediately suspect if the money in his pockets wasn't worn and dirty.

Identity cards, ration books, and other necessary papers were usually carefully counterfeited by being patterned after legitimate official documents stolen and smuggled out of occupied Europe. This was a process that called for not only great skill but also alertness and up-to-date knowledge of recent events in whatever country agents were to operate. Identity cards and passes into and out of certain European zones were occasionally recalled and new ones issued by Nazi authorities. A spy caught with an out-of-date pass was signing his or her own death warrant. A specific example of how even minor mistakes could backfire with deadly results was furnished not by the Allies but by the Germans during the Battle of the Bulge late in the war.

By the time the Battle of the Bulge occurred in December of 1944, the Germans had captured many American soldiers. Each of these GIs carried a U.S. military identification or AGO (for Adjutant General's Office) card. The first line on this card bore the soldier's name—Joseph E. Brown, for example. This seemed innocent enough. But if a soldier had no middle name, it was U.S. Army procedure to fill out that line: Joseph (NMN) Brown, indicating that Joseph Brown had No Middle Name. Every now and again the Germans would encounter such an entry in the AGO cards they took from American prisoners of war, and it puzzled them. The Germans, however, were nothing if not methodical, and when the time came to use this information they made doubly certain it was more than correct.

As part of their counterattack through the Ardennes forest in Belgium, which became known as the Battle of the Bulge, the Germans dressed a company of soldiers in American uniforms. These disguised men were supposed to infiltrate the American lines and help cause general confusion by misdirecting U.S. reinforcements and other military traffic. At the time of the Battle of the Bulge there was a story that these enemy agents were also assigned the task of invading Allied military headquarters and assassinating high-ranking officers, including General Dwight Eisenhower. This story, however, was never proved to be true. Nevertheless, these Germans in American uniforms did manage to add greatly to the overall confusion resulting from the surprise German attack. Just the knowledge of their presence behind the American lines was enough to make it mortally dangerous for a legitimate GI to appear unannounced on a legitimate mission in an area where he was unknown. Trigger-happy sentries were only too eager to shoot first and establish identities later.

In the opening days of the Battle of the Bulge, legitimate GIs stopped suspicious-looking GIs and asked them questions that probably only an American could answer—Babe Ruth's team and what his home-run record was, the identity of certain comic strip characters, the states in which certain cities were located, and so forth. But after the first false GIs were captured a means of identifying all other Germans disguised in American uniforms was quickly discovered. For each of these infiltrators had been furnished with a counterfeit AGO card that at first glance looked completely legitimate. The only flaw was that each AGO card bore not only the bearer's name in full, Herman B. Klaus, for example, but also the entry (NMN). Although they didn't understand what (NMN) stood for, the Germans had found it on a few captured AGO cards, so when it came time to equip their disguised agents with counterfeit AGO cards they decided to make doubly certain their counterfeits were accurate and up-to-date by providing that information on *all* of the cards. Thus, Herman B. Klaus, even though he had a middle name that was indicated by the letter *B*, carried an AGO card reading: Herman B. (NMN) Klaus.

With this information American Counterintelligence Corps (CIC) agents were able to round up all of the disguised German infiltrators within a few days. All were shot.

Behind the Lines

One of the most important jobs performed by both American and British agents dropped into occupied Europe was working with underground or resistance groups. These guerrilla organizations were called "Partisans" in Eastern Europe and the "Maquis" (*ma-kee*) in France and parts of Belgium. Partisans operated most effectively in Czechoslovakia, Yugoslavia, and even in Russia. In addition, it was disclosed long after the war that a relatively small but effective underground had existed inside Hitler's Germany at the height of World War II. The French underground, the Maquis or Maquisards, took its name from the low bushes called *maquis* that grew alongside many European roads and in which bandits could hide. The French also had several other resistance organizations including an important one called the French Forces of the Interior (FFI), which was nicknamed "The Fifi" (*fee-fee*). Generally, however, all French underground forces were simply grouped together and called the Resistance.

All of these resistance groups were constantly active in carrying on underground warfare against the occupying German troops. This warfare included sabotage, assassination, and in some instances direct and open combat.

Some of these forces were relatively large. One American agent from Illinois, Ernst Floeg, commanded a group of almost four thousand Maquis, and another agent, a French-born U.S. immigrant, Jacques Duval, both organized and led some seven thousand resistance fighters.

By the spring of 1944 when the Allies landed in France the entire Resistance had grown so large and become so active that it amounted to an underground government. Resistance groups even published their own newspapers and put out information bulletins to keep their members up-to-date as well as to boost their morale. One such bulletin bluntly stated the philosophy of the underground fighters. It said: "To terror there is no other reply than a more powerful terror. Assassination of any French patriot which is not immediately followed by the execution of those responsible for the crime or of another of their people is a dishonor for the Resistance."

The constant harassment of German occupation troops by members of the Resistance led to great insecurity on the part of the Nazi high command. A top German general, Field Marshal Gerd von Rundstedt, later called the Resistance "a tremendous threat to the fighting troops in France." When the Germans first occupied France, many of them went on sightseeing tours, but it wasn't long before sniper fire and plastic bombs put an end to this carefree activity. The Germans often overestimated the actual size of the Resistance forces, but their elusive presence in an area seriously demoralized the Nazi troops.

Among the key needs of the Resistance were weapons and ammunition. These were usually flown in and dropped by parachute. Once they were dropped, however, concealing them until they could be distributed became a tricky problem. One Maquis group solved this problem by temporarily concealing a supply of arms that had been dropped at night inside a church. The next day the local priest solemnly conducted a funeral ceremony and that

Military equipment, such as this light artillery piece,
was also parachuted to the Partisans and the French Resistance.

night the coffin that had been buried during the ceremony was dug up by the Maquisards and the cache of arms it contained retrieved and distributed.

All, however, was not—as the British put it—"fun and games" in playing the Resistance role, and casualties among the agents who led the resisters were extremely high. Records for all of the areas in which the American and British agents operated are sketchy at best, but those for occupied Belgium alone give an alarming indication of the overall mortality rate. Almost half of the 250 agents dropped into Belgium were captured and only 40 of these survived. Anyone consistently operating a shortwave radio —these were called "piano players" or "pianists"—could be expected to be captured within a few months. And capture was inevitably followed by the grimmest kind of physical torture in an effort to get an agent to disclose details of his or her work and thus "roll up" or destroy an entire underground network.

All agents carried a so-called L pill containing potassium cyanide as part of their field equipment. This, if placed in the mouth and chewed, brought death within minutes. Many agents, to avoid disclosing information during the tortures of interrogation, popped their L pill into their mouth when captured. If they were not tortured, the pill, which had an insoluble coating, could simply be swallowed with no ill effects.

By early 1943 some four hundred French-speaking Americans serving with the OSS had been dropped into France to aid the Resistance. These had been preceded by several hundred British agents. Overall casualties amounted to almost forty percent. They were soon followed by more than four hundred additional members of so-called Jedburgh teams, which were named for the geographical area in which they took their final training in Great Britain. The Jedburgh teams were made up of a Frenchman, an American, and a Briton. These men wore uniforms and thus technically were not agents. Their very existence, however, was kept secret, and if they were captured the fact that they were working with the Resistance was enough reason for the Germans to shoot them.

Hazardous as the role of the agent in occupied Europe was, it had its compensations for those freedom-fighters who believed they were risking their lives to prevent Hitler from turning back civilization's clock to the Dark Ages. One of these compensations came with the assassination of Reinhard Heydrich. Heydrich was called "The Hangman" and as chief of the secret state police, the *Gestapo,* was one of the most feared men in Germany. Heydrich was also deputy to Heinrich Himmler, head of the Nazi Security Service (SS), or *Schutzstaffeln.*

Early in the war Himmler and Heydrich, acting on what Hitler called his "final solution of the Jewish question," had marked out eleven million Jews for extermination. With his "Operation Reinhard," Heydrich was well on the road toward accomplishing this goal by 1941 with the killing of almost two million Jews at several extermination camps in Eastern Europe. "Operation Reinhard" was followed by a "Night and Fog" program, which called for the secret capture and disposal of all of those who opposed Nazi occupation troops—namely, all members of the Resistance.

Night and Fog was Heydrich's method of matching terror with terror in an attempt to put a halt to the guerrilla activities that were having such a serious effect on German troop morale. When Heydrich began to drop the deadly blanket of night and fog over not only captured members of the Resistance but also innocent civilians, British Intelligence decided to eliminate him.

Plans to assassinate Heydrich were made at BSC headquarters in New York. First, R&A was asked to provide complete background information about Heydrich, including where he was apt to be on certain given dates. It

*Partisans in Eastern Europe had to carry
on their guerrilla warfare under the most primitive conditions.
Here Partisans prepare a mountain redoubt with the aid of oxen.*

was learned that Heydrich, his wife, and their three children were living in a castle in Prague, Czechoslovakia. It was also learned, through Ultra intercepts, that Heydrich was scheduled to leave his home in Prague on a day in late May to visit Hitler in Berlin.

The personnel at the British Camp X in Canada then set about constructing an exact replica of the winding road leading from Heydrich's castle. This was done with the aid of still photographs and newsreel motion pictures furnished by Hollywood motion-picture director and key member of BSC Alexander Korda. Korda's pictures indicated that one of the hairpin turns in the castle road would be the ideal place for the assassination.

Nine men were then put through training to kill Heydrich. Of these, two were finally chosen for the job. They were Joseph Gabcik and Jan Kubris, natives of Prague who had escaped when the Germans first moved into Czechoslovakia but who now returned there after being dropped by parachute into a little town in nearby Poland. They made the rest of their way to Prague on foot.

On the morning of May 27, 1942, Gabcik and Kubris, armed with powerful automatic weapons and hand grenades supplied by the Czech underground, waited beside the hairpin bend. Acting as lookouts for them were two local Partisans, known only as Valcik and Jemelik. At the moment Heydrich's chauffeur-driven Mercedes touring car appeared far up the winding castle road, the two lookouts whistled sharply four times—the Morse code for *H.* In a few more minutes Heydrich's car—slowed by the sharp bend in the road—was in front of Gabcik and Kubris. Gabcik brought out his automatic weapon—a British Sten gun—from beneath his bulky overcoat, leveled it at Heydrich just a few yards away, and pressed the trigger. Nothing happened. The Sten gun had jammed. Heydrich now saw his assassins and shouted at his driver to speed up. Before the driver could do so, Kubris pulled the pin on a grenade and lobbed it at the Mercedes. It fell beside the car but then exploded and blasted the car and its occupants over on its side and into the ditch. Moments later Heydrich climbed out of one of the side doors, staggered a few paces, and then fell to the ground mortally wounded.

The two assassins hid in the crypt beneath a nearby church, having been taken there by other Partisans. While they were in hiding, more than ten thousand Czech hostages were ordered by Hitler to be taken from the civilian population of Prague. The two assassins remained at large for several days, despite a huge reward offered for their capture. And each day they remained at large Hitler ordered that one hundred of the Czech hostages be shot. Gabcik and Kubris never escaped from the church crypt. Informers reported their hiding place, and they were machine-gunned to death and the church burned to the ground.

Then the Germans learned that Gabcik and Kubris had been parachuted into a town called Lidice in Czechoslovakia at the start of their assassination mission. Lidice was also burned to the ground and all of its inhabitants—men, women, and children—were either shot, burned alive inside their homes, barns, and the local school building, sent to gas chambers, or sent to Berlin to be experimented on like human guinea pigs.

Many people thought the British and the Czech Partisans had asked the Czech people to pay too high a price for the assassination of Heydrich. But the German reprisals for Heydrich's death lit a flame of resistance in Eastern Europe that was not only never extinguished but also grew brighter all during the war. It was, in fact, a flame that grew throughout the free world. In the United States, for example, the people in towns in Illinois and New York renamed their communities Lidice, so the little Czech village would live on both in name and in spirit in America. After the war the city was completely rebuilt.

Because their people suffered such atrocities at the hands of the Germans—incidents similar to the total destruction of Lidice happened throughout the war, and the mass slaughter of Jews went on unabated—members of the Resistance throughout Europe were especially bitter toward members of their own country who collaborated with the Germans. By way of warning, many collaborators were sent tiny coffins in the mail. Lists were kept of those who continued to collaborate and when France and the rest of Europe were liberated by the Allies, mass retributions began. Some of these lists were even published in underground newspapers accompanied by the headline: Don't Forget to Hate!

A woman who collaborated with the Germans was lucky if she merely had her head shaved and was forced to march naked through her town's main streets. Many women and most men collaborators were summarily shot by their own countrymen. Before this mass purge of retribution could be brought to an end by France's leader-in-exile, General Charles de Gaulle, and other Allied commanders, as many as forty thousand collaborators were executed.

But before the Allied landings in Normandy and the liberation of Europe that followed, the Resistance did much other valuable work to pave the way for the eventual defeat of Germany. Much of this work had to do with the Allied mass aerial bombing attacks on Hitler's *Festung Europa*—Fortress of Europe.

Underground Railway for Airmen

Before the United States Army Eighth Air Force arrived in Great Britain in 1942, the Royal Air Force had been bombing Germany and occupied France for more than two years. During this period a number of RAF flyers were shot down, but not all were killed or taken prisoner. Many parachuted from their flak-battered planes before they crashed and then, having landed safely, fled before they could be captured by German army ground troops. Escaping from the immediate area was one thing, however. Escaping out of Germany or German-occupied territory and getting back to Great Britain was far more difficult. And this was where the Resistance movement or underground again moved into action.

Few of the first RAF flyers who parachuted to safety from shattered planes over continental Europe and tried to escape were successful. All, of course, were in flying gear and uniforms and thus easily recognizable. In addition, not many spoke French or German and as soon as they stopped at a house asking for help the occupants, fearing German reprisals, usually turned them over to the local Nazis. Occasionally, however, a family sympathetic to the Allied cause would take in "escapees," as they were

called by air force personnel, feed them, tend their wounds
if necessary, give them civilian clothing, and send them
on their way south toward Spain. If such a family had
friends or relatives in a nearby town, an escapee might be
told to stop at their house. Gradually a network of such
"safe" houses began to be built up, and those flyers who
successfully escaped from the Continent told their intelligence officers about the route they had followed to freedom. British agents working with the Resistance also became aware of this growing escapee network and worked
to expand it by using the homes of Resistance members
as safe houses. By the time the United States Eighth Air
Force began to lose flyers over Europe this underground
network to process escapees had attained the proportions
of the "Underground Railway" that helped slaves escape
from the South before the American Civil War. The Americans in Europe worked through their own intelligence
and counterintelligence operatives to further expand and
improve on this network.

One of the keys to maintaining this network was in not
letting anyone in the chain of safe houses know the location of more than one or at most two of the next safe houses
in their area. This made it impossible for someone who
hid escapees and was discovered to disclose the entire escape route and allow the network to be rolled up or destroyed. Keepers of safe houses who were caught were, of
course, executed by the Nazis. This was frequently done in
the local village square as a warning to other underground
members.

Before they left on a bombing mission Allied air crews
were briefed on escape procedures if they were shot down
over the Continent. They were also given a compact escape kit, which they carried in a pocket in a leg of their
flight coveralls. This kit contained concentrated survival
food, energy pills—usually some form of Benzedrine—a
sterilized antiseptic bandage pack, a compass of some sort,

*Agents took lonely nighttime drops like this
into enemy-occupied Europe.*

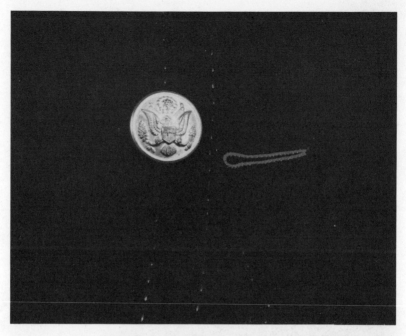

This ordinary-looking army uniform button (top) contained a hidden compass (bottom). By unscrewing the top of the button the concealed compass was revealed.

and an escape map. These last two items were of prime importance if a downed flyer hoped to make his way out of enemy-occupied territory.

First of all, a shot-down flyer had to know his directions if he wanted to head south. (There were no women combat flyers in World War II. A few women pilots ferried planes from factories where they were manufactured to training airfields.) This the compass told him. The compasses issued airmen did not resemble an ordinary compass. Some looked like a regular uniform button but a button whose top could be unscrewed to disclose a magnetic needle floating inside. Others looked like plain pen or pencil clips. These had their tips magnetized so that if the clip were balanced on a pencil point the tip would gradually swing in the direction of magnetic north. Escape maps were printed on silk so they could be folded into a small, compact rectangle. Each map clearly indicated rail and road networks that could be followed down into Spain. Safe houses were generally not shown on escape maps to prevent such knowledge falling into the hands of the Germans in case an escapee was captured. Before takeoff, however, airmen were briefed on the location of safe houses in the towns around that day's bombing mission and using this knowledge plus his compass and map a flyer could usually take the first step on his underground road back to freedom.

The journey to Spain was never an easy one. First of all, an escapee frequently had to lie hidden in an uncomfortable attic or cellar or barn for days before arrangements could be made to transport him to the next safe house. Sometimes he was carried in a farm cart, hidden beneath farm produce. Sometimes he had to walk, alone and at night and fearing capture along the way. Food was always scarce even for the local inhabitants and the escapee often had to go without food for much of his journey. Consequently, by the time he reached southern France he was

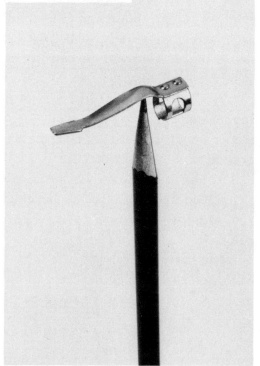

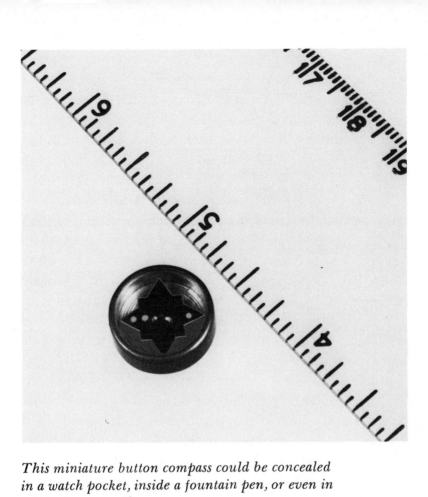

This miniature button compass could be concealed
in a watch pocket, inside a fountain pen, or even in
an escapee's mouth.

◀ (Left) What appeared to be a pencil clip was also a compass.
The magnetized tip of the clip would point north when the clip
was balanced on the tip of a pen or pencil.

usually near physical and emotional exhaustion. And it was right at that point that the most difficult part of his journey was about to begin. Now he had to cross the Pyrenees Mountains into Spain, and the rocky passes through the Pyrenees were difficult to find and more difficult to follow.

Spain was a neutral nation during World War II and thus technically could not take sides. General Francisco Franco, however, was Spain's dictator and was sympathetic toward the Axis powers. Nevertheless, there were numerous Basque peasants who were willing to lead escapees through the Pyrenees. For such work most expected a fee from American or British state department officials once an airman was delivered safely in Spain, but many did the work out of sheer loyalty to the Allied cause.

Because Spain was a neutral nation, once an escaping Allied flyer reached Spain he was taken into custody by the Spanish police and temporarily placed under arrest. Once this technicality was taken care of and a certain fee or ransom in gold was paid—at one point in the war Franco demanded a ransom of ten thousand dollars in gold per flyer, but this amount decreased with each Allied victory over the Germans—the escapee was set free and he was flown back to Great Britain in an American or British plane. There he was debriefed, his escape route checked, and then he was assigned to nonflying duty. American escapees were usually promoted one grade, given an air medal or some similar decoration, and returned to the United States. No escapee who made it safely back to England was allowed to fly over the Continent again for fear he might again be shot down, captured, and in being questioned disclose his earlier escape route.

One of the most difficult problems for the owner of a safe house on the underground route to face was sheltering a wounded Allied flyer. This happened not once but several times to Mr. and Mrs. Gunocente Lauro, who lived in the little French village of Lamorlaye north of Paris and near the racetrack town of Chantilly where the German *Luftwaffe* Fighter Command was located. The Lauros operated a safe house on the so-called Jeb Stuart network—named after the famed Civil War cavalry leader—which was one of the most successful underground routes. During the last several years of the war literally hundreds of Allied airmen escaped safely by being passed through the Lauro home and a dozen other safe houses on the Jeb Stuart underground network.

Mrs. Lauro had been born in England. While still a girl in her teens she had gone on a continental tour with a dance troupe. In Italy she had met and fallen in love with Gunocente, a trainer of racehorses. They were married and for several years she accompanied him when he took horses to the various race meetings throughout Europe. One of France's famous racetracks was at Chantilly, and the Lauros were at Chantilly when World War II began. Knowing that he would be conscripted into the Italian army if he returned to Italy, Gunocente decided that he and his wife should remain in France. When the Germans overran France and established their Fighter Command headquarters at Chantilly, Gunocente declared his nationality and told the Germans he wanted to work for them. He was put to work taking care of the few horses that the Nazi officers brought with them, and in his spare time served as a waiter in the officers' mess.

For some reason none of the German command seemed interested in the fact that Mrs. Lauro was a native of Great Britain. She spoke both French and Italian fluently and never spoke English in front of the Germans. In addition, her husband seemed completely loyal to the Nazis and they apparently assumed she must be also. In this they were completely wrong, for Mrs. Lauro had never lost her loyalty to Great Britain.

When the Germans took over all the living quarters in

Chantilly, the Lauros moved to nearby Lamorlaye. There they occupied a small, one-story home that had only a living room, bedroom, and kitchen. It was this modest home, however, that soon became one of the most important safe houses on the Jeb Stuart route of the escapee network.

The Lauros had not been in Lamorlaye long before Mrs. Lauro was approached by a local member of the Resistance. Despite her husband's violent opposition, she joined the local Resistance group immediately. Before there were escaping flyers to hide in her home, Mrs. Lauro took part in acts of sabotage in and around Chantilly. There were trains to Paris that could be derailed, trucks in the local German motor pool that could be put out of commission by pouring powdered graphite into cylinder heads, and numerous other ways to harass the Nazis. The graphite was supplied to her by the local high school chemistry teacher, and the local druggist supplied her with sulfuric acid. The acid she put to good use by prevailing upon her husband to sneak her into the storeroom of the German officers' mess in Chantilly. There she poured the acid over all of the stored food. This act she performed several times and was only prevented from doing so again by several vicious guard dogs the Germans put in the storeroom. Prevented from poisoning the food, Mrs. Lauro poisoned the guard dogs instead. She had a pet dog of her own that she loved dearly, but she did not regard the savage guard dogs as similar animals in any way. This last act, however, began to make the Germans suspicious of Gunocente, and he prevailed upon his wife to continue her activities elsewhere.

It was at about this time that the first escaping Allied flyers began being processed through her home, and this occupied most of her time. In a matter of months Mrs. Lauro had sheltered dozens of escapees, fed them, given them civilian clothes supplied by other members of the Resistance, and sent them on their way to the next safe house. By this time she had the operation down to a routine, a routine that was only broken by having to shelter wounded flyers who sometimes had to be kept in the small Lauro home for days at a time. Usually the local doctor, also a member of the Resistance, could come to the Lauro home late at night and patch up a slightly wounded escapee sufficiently for him to continue on his way. But badly wounded flyers were another story.

The incident Mrs. Lauro always remembered best—an incident she told to a member of air force counterintelligence after France was liberated—had to do with an American major who staggered into her home one evening with a serious wound in his thigh.

The major—Mrs. Lauro never exchanged names with her escapees so there would be no information to give the Germans if she or they were caught—was placed on a couch in the living room, and that night the doctor was summoned. He tended the American's wound but told Mrs. Lauro that if the major lived, and it was doubtful, he would not be able to travel for many weeks.

This situation was bad enough, but to make matters worse one of the local German officers had recently been coming to the Lauro home each evening to play checkers and drink wine with Gunocente. The Lauros did not know whether this was simply a friendly gesture or a means of keeping a close watch on Gunocente about whom the Nazis had become suspicious. In any event it greatly increased the possibility that the wounded American major would be discovered.

Fortunately, the German officer and Gunocente played checkers and drank their wine in the kitchen of the Lauro home. But there was no door, only a heavy curtain between the kitchen and the living room where the major lay on the couch. Any kind of noise from the living room while the German officer was in the kitchen could easily be heard. Mrs. Lauro made a particular point each evening of spending most of her time in the curtained-off living room, so that if there was a noise she could pretend she had made it. But groans or similar sounds would be difficult to explain. To solve this problem she began telling the German officer how sick her pet dog had been, so sick she was afraid the dog would die. This ruse worked well, for no matter how often she warned the convalescing American major of the German officer's presence, he still occasionally drifted off to sleep and in his sleep groaned or even snored. On these occasions Mrs. Lauro would hastily appear in the kitchen cradling her dog and exclaiming about its serious condition.

The American major remained in the Lauro home for six long weeks before he was able to travel further along the escape route. While he was there, Mrs. Lauro also sheltered and passed along several other escapees, and afterward she helped save the lives of dozens of others. But the badly wounded American major was always the one she remembered best; she was always deeply proud of the fact that she had probably saved his life. Or at least she hoped his life had been saved, since no keeper of a safe house ever really knew what happened to their escapees after they moved off in the night toward the next safe house on the network.

When France was liberated, Mrs. Lauro was asked if she wasn't grateful that the war was now almost over so that she and her husband could go back to living a peaceful way of life. "I shall be glad to have all the senseless killing come to an end, of course," she said. Then she smiled and added, "But I shall miss all of the excitement."

How America Helped Sink the *Bismarck*

United States flyers had actually been taking part in the air war against Germany long before America entered World War II. These flyers were not only young men who crossed the U.S. border into Canada and joined the Royal Canadian Air Force (RCAF) before Pearl Harbor, but also a handful of United States Navy pilots who flew amphibious aircraft, called "Catalina Flying Boats," for observation purposes with the British Royal Navy. The American RCAF volunteers were no particular secret; in fact, they later became part of a highly publicized group of combat flyers known as the Eagle Squadron. The fact that U.S. Navy pilots were flying with the British before Pearl Harbor was top secret, however. And the additional fact that one of these pilots played a key role in helping the British sink Germany's great battleship, the *Bismarck*, was one of the best kept secrets of the war. It was, in fact, an exploit that went unsung for more than thirty years after World War II.

In the spring of 1941 the German battleship *Bismarck* broke out into the north Atlantic from its hiding place in a Norwegian fjord. It was soon engaged in combat by several ships of the Royal Navy, including HMS *Hood,* regarded by many as the world's greatest battleship. By a combination of luck and expert German marksmanship the first salvo fired by the *Bismarck* scored a direct hit on the *Hood*'s top deck, penetrated the metal plating, and exploded the ship's main powder magazine. Within moments the mighty *Hood* had sunk with a loss of almost sixteen hundred officers and men. The *Bismarck* then disappeared into the mists of the North Atlantic, and the greatest search in the history of the Royal Navy began to find and destroy her. Aiding in the search were American Intelligence personnel and U.S. Navy flyers.

President Roosevelt thought that the loss of the *Hood* might also mean the eventual loss of the war for Great Britain. German submarines were already causing havoc with merchant vessels trying to supply the British Isles, and a German battleship like the *Bismarck* plus another equally formidable German warship, the *Prinz Eugen*, that could travel the oceans virtually at will could destroy all traffic in the shipping lanes. He was even afraid that the *Bismarck* might make its way across the Atlantic and bomb New York!

If the *Bismarck* were allowed to roam the seas unmolested, Roosevelt decided the situation might indeed become hopeless. Despite the Neutrality Act, which prohibited such actions, Roosevelt decided to give direct, short-of-war aid to the British in their attempt to find and sink the *Bismarck*. Once again he was committing an impeachable act.

This aid consisted of the use of eighty U.S. Navy Catalina PBYs, or flying boats, plus the men to fly them. Great Britain had no similar search planes in its Coastal Command, the air arm of the Royal Navy, and they were to prove invaluable. Several of these planes and their American pilots soon joined the search for the *Bismarck*. One of these pilots was a U.S. Navy farm boy from Missouri, Leonard Smith.

Smith was just one of literally thousands of airmen and sailors engaged in the massive search by British battle cruisers, destroyers, aircraft carriers, and torpedo bombers. Ashore, American and British agents were also feverishly engaged in trying to obtain and decipher Enigma's Ultra messages that might disclose the location and battle plans of the *Bismarck*. Nevertheless, the great German warship remained hidden for days.

All during this time Ensign Smith continued to fly search missions out of British Coastal Command's port of Londonderry in Northern Ireland. Finally, the British intercepted an Ultra message that indicated the *Bismarck* was trying to make its way to port in occupied France on the Bay of Biscay. If she made it there and came under the protection of the shore-based *Luftwaffe* aircraft, an attack on the *Bismarck* would be impossible.

Shortly after dawn on a cloudy May morning, Ensign Smith banked his Catalina on what was to be the final leg of that morning's square search. As he did so, through a small break in the overcast he thought he saw a ship beneath him. Unhesitatingly, he dropped his plane down to wave-top level. Almost immediately the warship's pom-pom guns opened fire on his slow-moving flying boat and antiaircraft flak began to burst around him. Fearful that he might be shot down before he could send his message, Smith immediately radioed:

BATTLESHIP BISMARCK LOCATED

He then added the nautical location of the *Bismarck* as well as his own. Having received acknowledgment that his message had reached naval operations in London, Ensign Smith banked his plane away from the deadly pom-pom gunfire and returned safely to Londonderry.

Forwarding the vital information from naval operations to the entire naval and air search forces took only moments.

Within hours Swordfish torpedo planes from the British aircraft carrier *Ark Royal* were dispatched and their attacks soon disabled the *Bismarck*'s steering mechanism. Finally, a British cruiser, the *Dorsetshire*, which had been alerted not by Royal Navy Operations in London but by Ensign Smith's original signal, moved in on the morning of May 27, 1941, and launched the torpedoes that sank the *Bismarck*.

Germany's Secret Vengeance Weapons

Almost as soon as the United States came into the war another intense search began for a mysterious secret weapon that Allied agents reported the Germans were working on. Information smuggled out of Germany finally indicated that this secret weapon was some sort of military rocket device, and that the experimental site for this rocket device was at Peenemünde on the Baltic Sea. This secret weapon was actually the V-2 rocket, a long-range, self-propelled missile carrying an explosive warhead. This device, together with the V-1 flying bomb or "buzz bomb" (the *V* stood for Vengeance, a name supplied by Hitler), came very close to changing the entire course of the war.

The Treaty of Versailles after World War I had prohibited Germany from producing military guns, artillery cannon, and similar weapons. It said nothing, however, about the development and production of military rockets. Between the two world wars the Germans took advantage of this treaty oversight when Army General Walter Dornberger selected civilian engineer Wernher von Braun to develop rockets for military use.

The use of rockets in warfare dated back to the early Chinese who used them against the Mongols as early as the thirteenth century. Their first important use, however, was by the British in the nineteenth century. These were large rockets with explosive warheads developed by artillery Captain William Congreve. Congreve rockets bursting over Baltimore's Fort McHenry in the War of 1812 were what inspired Francis Scott Key to write "The Star Spangled Banner."

These early rockets, however, and those used right up to World War II were all fueled by black powder, which was so weak it would only carry a rocket a few thousand yards. Artillery could do a better, more reliable job. Between the two world wars experiments with the use of smokeless powder were carried on which were successful. And on March 16, 1926, an American inventor, Dr. Robert Goddard, made the first successful test of a liquid-fuel rocket.

Von Braun and his team of engineers used all of the most recent knowledge about new rocket fuels in their experiments at Peenemünde. Their first experiments were with rockets to be used by aircraft in rocket-assisted take-offs. When these were successful—they eventually led to the development of the fully jet-powered plane—work began on the V-2, a rocket that would carry a two-ton warhead. Hitler himself saw the first test of the V-2 in March 1939. He was not impressed. The V-2 was so erratic in flight that the men who launched it seldom knew when or where it would land. Nevertheless, Dornberger continued work on the V-2, secretly employing more than twelve hundred army engineers to aid von Braun on the project. On October 3, 1942, the V-2 was first successfully launched, but work continued to perfect its occasionally erratic flight.

Meanwhile, reports from agents had continued to flow out of Europe about the work at Peenemünde, and Danish fishermen also reported on the important activity there. RAF reconnaissance planes regularly took photographs of the area, but it was not until 1943 that aerial photos disclosed hard evidence of Germany's actual secret weapon—

a missile resting on a launching ramp. On the night of August 17, 1943, the RAF sent three hundred bombers to destroy the place. Later American planes also bombed the area. But these raids were too late. Most of the above-ground facilities were destroyed, but production had already begun underground on not only the V-2 rocket but also the V-1 flying bomb.

The V-1 resembled a miniature plane more than it did a rocket. It was developed by the *Luftwaffe* when the German air force grew impatient with the army's slow progress on the V-2. The V-1, or small rocket plane, carried a one-ton load of explosives in its fuselage. The rear of the fuselage contained an automatic pilot, and the engine's fuel supply was carried on top of the fuselage. The V-1 flew at low altitudes—seldom more than 2,000 feet (600 m)— at a speed of about 350 miles (560 km) per hour. It could travel about 150 miles (240 km), and when its fuel was exhausted the V-1 fell to the ground and exploded on impact. It was clearly visible and audible in flight, looking like a small, pilotless plane and emitting a kind of *put-put-put* sound from its pulse jet engine. Because of their curiously jerky flight, the British frequently called the V-1s "Doodlebugs."

The V-2, or long-range rocket, on the other hand, could neither be seen nor heard until it hit the ground and its warhead exploded much like a large aerial bomb. The V-2 worked somewhat like an elaborate skyrocket, being launched in a high arc to a height of more than 20 miles (32 km). Traveling more than twice as fast as the speed of sound, its liquid-fueled propellant carried it a distance of about 200 miles (320 km).

Despite every effort on the part of Allied Intelligence teams as well as the Allied air forces, mass production of both the V-1 and V-2 had reached a peak by 1944. Allied bombing efforts and sabotage by Allied agents did, however, succeed in delaying the launching of these Vengeance weapons until two weeks after the successful Normandy landings on D-Day, June 6, 1944. Had they been launched earlier, the D-Day landings would probably not have been possible. As it was, once the Allies were ashore and had liberated key cities and ports, two thousand Vengeance weapons were launched against one of the main Allied liberated ports, Antwerp, virtually destroying it.

The first of more than eight thousand V-1 flying bombs launched against Britain hit London in late June of 1944. In all, about twenty-five hundred of these actually hit the city. The rest were either shot down by fighter aircraft alerted by Allied Intelligence messages or by antiaircraft batteries. A few hit barrage balloons stationed at the city's perimeter or fell short or overshot their target. The attacks continued for several months until the V-1 launching sites were captured along the Channel coast by the advancing Allied armies. The V-1s caused between forty thousand and fifty thousand casualties.

The first V-2 long-range rockets were launched from the Netherlands against Great Britain on September 8, 1944. They continued to rain down death and destruction until March of the following year when the Allies captured the areas where they were being manufactured. Capturing the V-2 launching sites was not possible, since they could be launched from beds on rail flatcars that could be moved about at will until the entire German rail network was destroyed. In all, more than twelve hundred V-2s hit Britain out of fourteen hundred fired, causing some ten thousand casualties.

Despite the fact that the V-2s caused far fewer casualties than the V-1s, Britons feared the long-range V-2 rockets far more than they did the flying bombs, mainly because the V-2s arrived silently and no one was aware of their presence until suddenly an entire building or city square might erupt from a V-2 explosion.

As the Allies overran occupied Western Europe and

One of Hitler's Vengeance weapons, a V-1 robot bomb,
that did not explode but landed intact.

Germany itself, the threat of the Vengeance weapons ended as abruptly as it began, and with Allied victory in Europe the "Little Blitz" the V-1s and V-2s created became a bad memory to be compared by survivors with the "Big Blitz" at the start of the war. Only a few knowledgeable Allied Intelligence people really shuddered with relief when the last V-1 and V-2 hit Great Britain. What, they wondered, would have happened if the Vengeance weapons had been equipped with nuclear warheads? For the Germans had come close to accomplishing this feat also, and Allied Intelligence agencies knew it. But the successful development of an atomic bomb was to be first accomplished by the United States for use against Japan.

Interestingly and somewhat ironically, after the Allies took over Peenemünde and the war was almost ended both General Dornberger and Wernher von Braun plus more than 125 Germans who had headed the Vengeance weapons team arrived in the United States to work on the American military nuclear rocket program as well as on the peacetime space plans. Thus, in a major way, development of the Vengeance weapons eventually led to man's first landing on the moon.

Japan's Aerial Bombardment of the United States

Within a matter of a very few hours after the Japanese air attack on Pearl Harbor, Hawaii, on December 7, 1941, the entire west coast of the United States was put on a military alert. Soldiers in the numerous west coast training camps were issued live ammunition for their weapons and soldiers on weekend passes or furloughs were ordered immediately to return to camp. Los Angeles, San Francisco, and other west coast cities that were under the jurisdiction of the Third Interceptor Command were subjected to sudden nightly blackouts when operators of primitive radar sets in the coastal highlands detected or thought they detected unidentified aircraft on their radarscopes.

This kind of mindless panic continued for days and, in some areas, even weeks until both the military organizations and civilian populace began to realize that a Japanese invasion was not about to take place nor was the west coast about to be subjected to aerial bombardment like that at Pearl Harbor. The most serious false alert occurred early on the morning of February 25, 1942, when Los Angeles antiaircraft batteries fired fourteen hundred rounds of artillery shells at nonexistent enemy aircraft. The next day Los Angeles newspapers reported the "air raid" in banner headlines, and it wasn't until many years later that an official War Department history admitted there had been no air raid on Los Angeles, but to have said so frankly at the time "would have meant a complete revelation of the weakness of our air defenses."

Commenting on this period, U.S. Army Sergeant William Campbell, who had been in charge of one of the Third Interceptor Command's early radar units, later said: "We probably caused more casualties from automobile accidents during a single blackout than would have been caused by a major air raid."

But the United States had been so suddenly and violently thrust into the war that a certain amount of hysteria was perhaps excusable. And it was partly because of this early hysteria that civilian government and military officials later decided to clamp a tight security lid on all information about the incidents that occurred when Japan actually did begin to bomb the United States. This was one of the best kept secrets of the war.

The Japanese were well aware of what devastating effects forest fires could cause in the Pacific Northwest's vast timber tracts, and soon after the war began they made plans to set fire to the hundreds of thousands of acres of trees in the Siskiyou National Forest. In September 1942 a Japanese aircraft was catapulted from the deck of one of Japan's unique—neither the Americans nor the British had such a vessel—aircraft-carrying submarines lying just off the Oregon coast. This aircraft dropped several incendiary (fire) bombs in the forest. Only one of the bombs started a fire among the wet trees, and it was quickly extinguished by forest rangers.

The Japanese high command then decided that its submarine aircraft carriers were needed elsewhere in the Pacific and assigned several ordinary submarines to duty off the Oregon coast. It was planned to launch balloons carrying incendiary bombs from these submarines, but before this plan could be put into effect the Imperial Navy also recalled its regular submarines for duty closer to the Japanese home islands. Army and air force engineers in Tokyo then began to consider other means of dropping bombs on the United States.

As far back as the 1920s Japanese military scientists had been studying the possibility of launching high-altitude balloons into the upper air currents and letting them drift in the jet stream as far as the United States. Now, Army Major General Sueki Kusaba and Navy Lieutenant Commander Kiyoshi Tanaka were put in charge of the project to bomb America through the use of incendiary and explosive bombs carried to their targets by high-altitude balloons.

General Kusaba and Commander Tanaka enlisted the aid of university professors, inventors, scientists, and their nation's major manufacturers to help them with their project. The results of their efforts were two types of balloons, one made of paper and the other rubberized silk, that could attain an altitude of more than 30,000 feet (9,100 m)—out of the normal range of fighter aircraft, antiaircraft fire, and even radar. Beneath each balloon would be a cluster of five incendiary and explosive bombs. After the balloon was in the air for a certain length of time —presumably long enough for the balloon to drift over the United States—a timing device would release the bombs, which would explode and burst into flame on impact. Another timing device would then explode the balloon so there would be no evidence remaining to indicate where the bombs had come from.

The success of these hydrogen-filled, bomb-carrying balloons was remarkable considering the fact that they were launched in Japan and then with neither a motor nor rudder made their way across the Pacific to the United States. So successful were they, in fact, that President Harry Truman, according to some historians, made his final decision to drop the atomic bomb on Japan to stop the balloon-bomb attacks on the United States. This, however, is doubtful since the attacks were gradually coming to an end before the atom-bombing of Hiroshima and Nagasaki. Nevertheless, they were a dangerous and worrisome menace during most of the last year of the war.

Because the balloons and their bombing mechanism were so difficult to perfect, the first bomb-laden balloons were not launched until late in 1944. In December of that year on the anniversary of the Pearl Harbor attack one exploded near Thermopolis, Wyoming. Although it caused no damage, it did cause a considerable amount of dismay when fragments of the bomb were identified by military demolition experts as Japanese.

News about the incident was quickly suppressed under wartime censorship regulations, and U.S. military intelligence and counterintelligence teams began to try and solve the mystery.

Within the next few weeks there were nineteen such bombing incidents in five western states, making it perfectly clear that Japan was attacking the United States with some mystery weapon. But what was its purpose? Intelligence experts at first thought that some form of biological warfare must be involved. It was only after the bomb fragments proved to be germ-free that the experts came to the conclusion that the purpose of the bombs was to set forests afire and kill civilians. But how were they being delivered? Finally, a Japanese balloon that had failed to self-destruct was recovered near Yerington, Nevada, and the answer became clear. But the problem of how to prevent the continued bombardment never was solved.

Between December 1944 and the end of the war the Japanese launched between six thousand and ten thousand high-altitude balloons carrying more than thirty thousand bombs. It took these balloons about seventy-two

A Japanese bomb-carrying balloon that failed to self-destruct and landed intact near Farmington, Washington.
This picture was kept secret until censorship was relaxed after World War II ended.

hours to reach the west coast of the United States where they dropped their bombs over a widespread area—at such places as Portland and Medford, Oregon; Goldendale, Washington; Sebastopol and Alturas, California, as well as in the California coastal waters and in such inland western states as Utah, Texas, Arizona, and Colorado. Some even traveled as far east as Kansas, Iowa, and Nebraska, and the one that traveled farthest east landed at Grand Rapids, Michigan. In addition, about one hundred bombs were dropped in Canada and Alaska, and several balloons that had malfunctioned and descended to fighter plane pursuit levels were shot down by American and Royal Canadian Air Force fighter pilots. In all, bombs hit twenty-six states and Canadian provinces and several additional ones fell as far south as Mexico.

None of the hundreds of bombs that actually exploded or burst into flame set any major forest fires during the year that Japan carried on its aerial bombardment of the United States. This was mainly because most of the bombs fell during the winter when the timber tracts were wet with rain and snow. The only bomb known to have killed anyone fell near Bly, Oregon, on May 5, 1945. On that day a minister's wife and five Sunday school students were having a picnic in the woods on the slope of Gearhart Mountain when they encountered an unexploded aerial bomb lying in a forest clearing. In examining the bomb one of the children accidentally detonated it and all six members of the picnic party were killed.

The Japanese gradually ended their aerial attacks on the United States partially because of the fact that one of the balloon factories in Tokyo was destroyed by an American B-29 raid. Mainly, however, it was because the Japanese never knew whether any of their balloons and their deadly cargo had actually reached the United States. The FBI and U.S. Intelligence and Counterintelligence services kept such a tight security lid on all of the bombing incidents that almost no information about them leaked out, causing the Japanese military high command to become discouraged with the project. Thus silence did indeed prove to be the best wartime policy.

American Concentration Camps

The fear that stalked the west coast of the United States immediately after Pearl Harbor had far more serious consequences than the mere nightly blacking out of cities because of suspected Japanese air raids. The fear led to the establishment of American concentration camps in which to intern Americans of Japanese ancestry. Because the United States prided itself that it was taking part in a just and righteous war in Europe by attempting to defeat an evil enemy who put millions of Jews in concentration camps, little or nothing was said when similar action was taken against the Japanese-Americans in the United States. The only difference was that the American camps were not used for the extermination of prisoners; but they were concentration camps nonetheless. Wartime secrecy, press censorship, and a conspiracy of silence on the part of those who were active participants kept this unsavory story quiet for many years, and full details were not disclosed until the mid-1970s.

When World War II began there were about 130,000 Japanese-Americans in the United States, most of whom lived in the states bordering the Pacific Ocean. These were divided into those who were Japanese born (*Issei*) and their children or second-generation Americans (*Nisei*). Most of the Issei and Nisei were truck farmers in California and were hard working, industrious, and frugal members of their farm communities. By the start of World War II they controlled about half of California's commercial truck crops, even though they numbered only one percent of the state's population.

Nevertheless, when war broke out a hysterical hue and cry was raised demanding that all of these Japanese-Americans be moved out of their homes and farms and places of business bordering the Pacific and into the interior. Some unscrupulous businessmen saw this as an excellent opportunity to eliminate these people from business and farming competition. The usual reason given, however, for this demand was to prevent subversion and sabotage such as the Japanese, it was claimed, had been guilty of at Pearl Harbor in Hawaii. Actually, such subversion in Hawaii was much less important than the failure of U.S. Naval Intelligence security precautions. In addition, a special representative of the U.S. State Department, Curtis B. Munson, agents from the FBI and U.S. Naval Intelligence all investigated the Japanese on the west coast and reported that there was no need for such an evacuation—in fact, they said, the Japanese living there were extremely loyal to the United States.

But the hysteria continued. Earl Warren, then Attorney General of California and later Chief Justice of the United States Supreme Court, stated: "The very fact that no sabotage has taken place to date is a disturbing and confirming indication that such action will be taken." By this nonsensical statement Warren apparently meant that everybody knew that it was just a matter of time until the west coast Japanese committed acts of sabotage. Oregon's Governor Charles Sprague wired Washington requesting "more thorough action for protection against possible alien activity, particularly by Japanese residing on coast." And

Seattle, Washington, Mayor Earl Milliken admitted that most of his city's Japanese were "probably above question" but a few "would burn this town down and let the Japanese planes come in and bring on something that would dwarf Pearl Harbor."

Washington officials also began to urge President Roosevelt to evacuate the west coast Japanese despite the fact that such a move would be unconstitutional. These officials included Secretary of War Henry L. Stimson, Secretary of the Navy Frank Knox, and General Dwight Eisenhower's brother, Milton Eisenhower, who later headed the War Relocation Authority that oversaw the American concentration camps.

Finally, on February 19, 1942, President Roosevelt issued Executive Order #9066 authorizing the evacuation of the west coast Japanese-American population. This order got around the legal problem of interning American citizens by permitting the Secretary of War to designate certain parts of the country as military areas from which certain people could be excluded. Congress later passed a law making it a federal offense to violate orders issued by a military commander in a military area.

The evacuation of all west coast Japanese-Americans began almost immediately. They were first moved out of their homes to assembly points. One of these assembly points, that for the Oregon Japanese, was the Portland stockyards. From here and other points the evacuees were herded together and shipped to twelve permanent inland concentration camps in Arizona, California, Colorado, Idaho, Utah, and Wyoming.

In the panic that resulted from this action many evacuees sold their homes, farms, and businesses at a fraction of their true value. Several older *Issei* committed suicide rather than face living behind barbed wire in what the government called "relocation centers." Many lost their life savings. The savings of four thousand depositors in the

Japanese-Americans arriving at an internment camp at Manzanar, California.

Japanese-American kindergarten children at an internment camp in Arkansas.

California branch of a Yokohama bank, for example, were seized by the United States as "enemy property." It was not until 1969, more than a quarter of a century after Pearl Harbor, that those investors or their families who were still living had their money returned—without interest. Also long after the war those Japanese-Americans who lost their land, businesses, and personal property were also repaid for these losses—at a rate of ten cents on each dollar of their assessed worth at the time the property was seized.

By 1944 most of President Roosevelt's advisers had reversed their earlier stand and were urging him to abolish the American concentration camps. Roosevelt, however, was running for reelection and the Japanese-American problem was politically a ticklish one—a national opinion poll indicated that forty-one percent of the American people still thought all Japanese people would "always want to go to war to make themselves as powerful as possible."

In order not to lose any votes, Roosevelt avoided the Japanese-American issue and consequently the unfortunate and innocent victims of this flagrant violation of civil rights were allowed to remain interned until the war ended.

Another Japanese-American who was dealt with harshly and, Americans generally agree, unfairly was California-born Iva Toguri, who became famous to U.S. soldiers throughout the Pacific in World War II as a Japanese propaganda broadcaster and disc jockey known as Tokyo Rose. The truth about Tokyo Rose—that there was not just one such broadcaster but several and that Iva Toguri actually broadcast using the name "Orphan Annie"—was not fully disclosed until long after the war.

Ironically, Iva Toguri was born on Independence Day, the Fourth of July, in 1916 in Los Angeles. After graduating from the University of California at Los Angeles

*"Tokyo Rose" as she looked when her trial
for treason began in San Francisco in 1949.*

with a degree in zoology, she went to Japan to visit a sick relative and war broke out before she could return home. Virtually alone in what was to her an alien land and pressured by Japanese authorities, she finally agreed to make daily English-language broadcasts on the "Zero Hour." The purpose of the broadcasts was to combine the playing of popular music with pleasant patter that would lower the morale of American GIs by making them homesick.

Under the name Orphan Annie, Iva Toguri was one of several women announcers used by Japanese-controlled radio stations in fourteen locations scattered throughout Asia and the Pacific. American soldiers, however, immediately applied the name Tokyo Rose to all of the women heard on Japanese radio. Actually, from the Japanese viewpoint, the broadcasts were a total failure. Instead of destroying morale they had a tendency to boost it, since the GIs regarded Tokyo Rose more with amusement and affection than anything else. And, as more than one GI put it, "She sure did play good American pop music. And where else could we hear it?"

But after the war when the American public's temper was still inflamed against Japan and American citizens of Japanese ancestry, U.S. occupation forces in Japan arrested Iva Toguri as the legendary Tokyo Rose. She was imprisoned in Tokyo for more than a year—without being charged, without a lawyer, and without trial. The U.S. Justice Department finally agreed that there was no case against her, and she was released in 1946. But when she applied to return to her homeland, the United States, in 1947, American newspapers and radio mounted a campaign against her as a traitor who had never been brought to justice. In 1948 she was again arrested and ordered to stand trial in San Francisco.

Iva Toguri's trial was one of the longest and most expensive on record, and at the end of it the jury reported it was deadlocked. Reminded by the judge of how expen-

*"Tokyo Rose" as she looked when she was pardoned by
President Gerald Ford in 1977.*

sive the trial had been, the jury finally found her guilty on one of eight counts. She was sentenced to ten years imprisonment and fined ten thousand dollars. The conviction took away Iva Toguri's American citizenship.

When she was released from prison in 1956 with time off for good behavior, the persecution of Iva Toguri continued. An attempt was made to deport her, and when this failed she was classified as a "stateless person." Later the federal government confiscated her life insurance policies to pay her fine. A true alien but still loyal to the United States, Iva Toguri worked for many years in an Oriental shop in Chicago. Several appeals for review of her case were denied by the U.S. Supreme Court, and two petitions for pardon by the president of the United States were ignored. Finally, however, as one of his last acts in office in January of 1977 President Gerald Ford issued a full and unconditional pardon to Tokyo Rose.

When the pardon was announced and Iva Toguri's picture was again back in the newspapers and on television, many an aging GI who had been a young man when serving in the Pacific during World War II blinked in wonderment at this grandmotherly looking little woman. Could this be the glamorous and romantic-sounding Tokyo Rose who had filled the long, dark nights with lovely fantasies of home and loved ones with her soft, young, all-American-girl voice and those beautiful pop records? When she was pardoned, Tokyo Rose was more than sixty years old.

XIV

Wartime Propaganda and Censorship

The Allies used completely different propaganda methods from those used by the Axis powers in World War II. Neither the United States nor Great Britain, for example, employed someone like Tokyo Rose to broadcast to enemy troops. But the Germans used the same technique as the Japanese with a young woman broadcaster whom both the British and Americans called "Axis Sally." Axis Sally was actually an American woman named Mildred Gillars. Like Iva Toguri, Mildred Gillars was sentenced to prison and served twelve years for broadcasting propaganda from Berlin during World War II. The Germans also used a man to broadcast propaganda in English early in the war. This broadcaster—the British laughingly referred to him as "Lord Haw Haw"—was a turncoat Englishman named William Joyce, who was eventually jailed by the British.

Actually propaganda, by its very nature, was not a part of the secret war. Censorship, however, was. Many people often thought of propaganda and censorship as being the same thing. They were not. At most they were two sides of the same coin.

Propaganda was used to publicize the war effort. Censorship protected military security by keeping troop movements, battle plans, and all similar information secret. For example, the U.S. Office of War Information, which was in charge of American propaganda efforts, issued many news stories about the war. The U.S. Office of Censorship never did. In fact, press censors often suppressed news stories. For example, when a new fighter aircraft such as the P-51 Mustang first was used in a combat zone. reporters were not allowed to mention the fact in press dispatches until at least three of the Mustangs had been shot down over enemy territory. This was to prevent the enemy from learning any details about the plane's combat capabilities. Once three were shot down it was assumed that the enemy had gained all the information it needed from the plane's wreckage.

Some press censorship was voluntary—that is, newspaper editors and radio station managers agreed not to mention anything about certain subjects in their newspapers or broadcasts. Voluntary censorship was generally practiced in the case of the Japanese balloon bombing of the United States as well as in the development of the atom bomb.

Propaganda used all means possible—newspaper, radio, wall posters, leaflets dropped from planes, motion pictures, dramatic plays—to convince citizens and military personnel alike that their side was winning the war and that the enemy side was losing. In addition, both sides used propaganda efforts to prove their side was "right." To accomplish these goals the Allied and Axis powers used different techniques in their propaganda efforts.

While certainly not secret, the Axis techniques and especially those used by Germany were completely deceptive and deceitful. They included every devious propaganda means possible to deceive both the German people and their enemies.

Joseph Goebbels was the mastermind behind all of Germany's propaganda. He and Hitler both believed that "the

"Is This Our War?"

by

CLAY JUDSON

of the

AMERICA FIRST COMMITTEE

★

Delivered before the

Chicago Bar Association

SATURDAY, NOVEMBER 30, 1940

★

AMERICA FIRST COMMITTEE

National Headquarters

1806 BOARD OF TRADE BUILDING · CHICAGO

<u>This</u> Mother's Day, May 11
Make it a <u>real</u> Mother's Day—
Do something for your son — our sons —

MOTHERS!

SEND THIS

S·O·S

SAVE   OUR   SONS

to President Roosevelt
Washington, D. C.

DEMAND! Pledges Be Kept.
DEMAND! No Foreign Wars.
DEMAND! No Convoys
DEMAND! No War
DEMAND! Save Our Sons

Let each of us—ask three other Mothers to write the President. Let's make <u>this</u> Mother's Day mean something. ALL mail should reach the President's desk on or before Mother's Day, Sunday, May 11.

AMERICA FIRST COMMITTEE
(Chapter Headquarters for ILLINOIS and IOWA)
122 South Michigan Avenue, Chicago, Illinois

★

To enter the wars now raging in Europe, Asia and Africa would be an act of national folly from which our country must be spared!

★

AMERICA FIRST COMMITTEE
1806 Board of Trade Building
CHICAGO, ILLINOIS

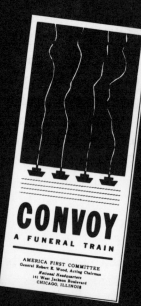

CONVOY
A FUNERAL TRAIN

AMERICA FIRST COMMITTEE
General Robert E. Wood, Acting Chairman
National Headquarters
141 West Jackson Boulevard
CHICAGO, ILLINOIS

bombardment of people's minds with propaganda is almost as important as the bombardment by cannon." When the war began, Goebbels was in complete control of all of Germany's newspapers, books, radio, drama, motion pictures, and the creative arts. *All* media were filled with pro-Hitler, pro-Nazi propaganda. As the war progressed, Goebbels expanded his propaganda techniques into German-occupied countries as well as against enemy countries.

Goebbels in his propaganda did not tell complete lies. These would have been discovered. But he did tell subtle and partial lies that eventually built into the "Big Lie." The Big Lie disguised Germany's true goals. "The sole aim of propaganda," Goebbels said, "is success. Let the professors of history discover historical truth. We are serving historical necessity."

The Nazis, for example, believed that all Germans—with the exception of German Jews—were a master race destined to rule Europe and eventually the world. Goebbels, however, said in his propaganda that Germany believed in European culture and society and that the only purpose of the war was to allow all people in all countries to share equally in all material and cultural things. This, Goebbels said, was simply to be a "New Order" of society in Europe. Although the Nazis themselves intended to conquer and rule Europe, Goebbels said in his propaganda that Germany was saving Europe from a variety of threats —Communists, Jews, and blacks.

The Allies, on the other hand, attempted to use a more

◀ *Isolationist organizations such as the America First Committee campaigned against the United States' entry into World War II right up to the attack on Pearl Harbor. Literature such as this appealed strongly to people's emotions. The S.O.S. "Save Our Sons" appeal to mothers on Mother's Day was especially effective.*

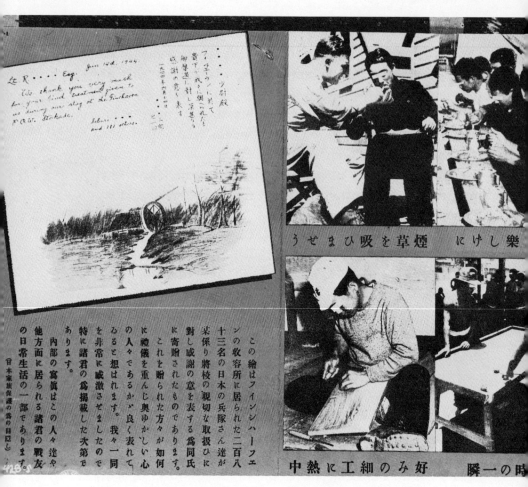

The U.S. Office of War Information prepared this leaflet to drop behind Japanese lines. Its message is an attempt to persuade Japanese soldiers to surrender because they are losing the war.

direct and open method of propaganda. Allied peacetime goals of no territorial demands in Europe were made known to all of the Axis people via all possible means of communication. Allied goals also included the destruction of nazism, fascism, and all forms of totalitarianism to be replaced by a world of free peoples. During the course of the conflict Allied propaganda gave essentially accurate results of the war's progress—bombing results, battle results, manpower, economic conditions, and every other kind of information that could possibly be given without endangering the immediate war effort.

While propaganda was an open effort to conduct what amounted to bloodless psychological warfare, censorship was an effort to conduct a form of secret bloodless warfare.

There were two kinds of American wartime censorship. The United States Office of Censorship was headed by Byron Price. It was entirely a civilian organization. It censored the press and radio; mail into and out of the United States; telegraph messages, cables, telephone calls, and any other means of communication with foreign nations. It attempted to build a wall of security around the United States and all of its military operations so that the enemy could gain no information that would endanger the American war effort.

The United States Army and Navy had their own mail censorship operation. In the army officers were assigned the task of reading and censoring enlisted men's mail. Officers themselves initialed their own letters to indicate that they contained no military or other classified information. Enlisted men were also issued so-called Blue Letters or Blue Envelopes—sometimes one a week but usually less frequently—in which they could mail correspondence that would not be read by their own officers. However, Blue Envelopes and officers' mail were all subject to censorship at a central military base. Navy officers' mail was subject to censorship by unit censors, and the navy enlisted men received no Blue Envelopes. Otherwise the systems were the same.

Military postal censorship was almost wholly effective —most members of the military regarded it as a point of honor not to divulge military secrets—and little of a dramatic nature occurred in the military censorship area during the war. The civilian Office of Censorship, however, produced some of the most important and dramatic results of any of the wartime organizations.

Bermuda was a central point for censoring much of the mail that flowed between Europe and North and South America. The British had established a major censorship operation there long before the United States entered the war. After Pearl Harbor this became a joint Anglo-American effort. Literally hundreds of thousands of letters and packages were opened and read as they passed through Bermuda. Some of this censorship was done openly, but much was done secretly. Censors—most of them women— became extremely efficient in opening envelopes, reading their contents, and resealing the envelopes so swiftly and efficiently that a letter's recipient was completely unaware that a censorship operation had been performed. Much intelligence information to and from agents in this hemisphere and abroad was gained in this way. An important early discovery was the use by Axis agents of the microdot or microphotography to send information secretly.

The microdot, invented by the Germans, was a way of concealing a message. By means of a special camera a single page of correspondence could be shrunk to the size of a pencil or pen dot. These microdots carrying military or other secret information could be placed over a punctuation mark in a regular letter and fastened to it with transparent adhesive. The person receiving the letter could remove the microdot or dots and their secret message could be read through a microscope. If a photographic labora-

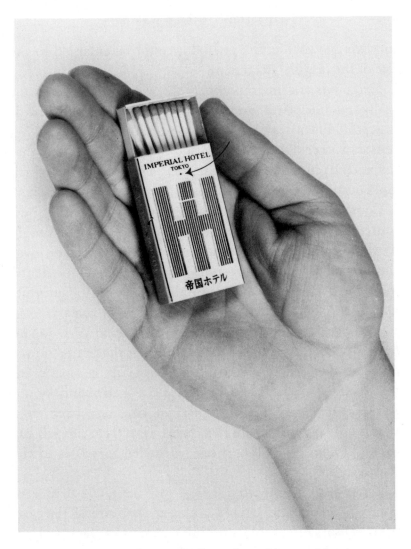

Microdots, such as the one indicated on this matchbox, were extremely difficult to detect.

tory were available, the microdot could be enlarged to the size of the original document.

Microdots and microphotographs went undiscovered for many months. And even when they were discovered it was still difficult to find them. Nevertheless, painstaking censors succeeded in intercepting a number of them that led directly to the capture of Axis agents in both North and South America.

Censorship was also responsible for discovering new sources of essential war materials that were in short supply or wholly unavailable because the enemy had taken over the areas where these materials were produced. One of the most important of these materials was the drug quinine. Quinine was needed as a medicine to treat malaria contracted by Allied troops fighting in the Pacific War. Japan, however, had taken over the East Indies, the major source of the drug. By carefully scanning the mails, censors eventually discovered that drug firms in Latin and South America had available stockpiles of cinchona bark from which quinine is made. These firms were trying to sell the bark elsewhere, but they were persuaded to sell it to the United States.

There were about fifty critical raw materials that were not available in the United States at the start of the war. Alert censors discovered stockpiles of most of them in Central and South America where German agents were also doing their best to obtain them for the Axis or to prevent anybody else from getting them. These materials ranged all the way from quartz crystals for electronic equipment to balsa wood for light observation planes and gliders to mahogany for the hulls of PT boats and even to special types of sponges needed for certain kinds of engine filters.

Weather was another thing the Office of Censorship had to worry about. It was essential that the enemy not receive accurate weather reports or forecasts from wide-ranging areas because this would enable enemy meteorologists to predict weather conditions elsewhere—in vital military combat zones, for example. Accurate weather forecasts were also invaluable to enemy submarines and aircraft operating off Allied coastlines. Consequently, weather reports were either eliminated throughout the United States and Great Britain or so heavily censored that they were of little value to either friend or enemy. As more than one newspaper feature writer pointed out, during wartime even the groundhog's activities each spring in predicting the weather were censored!

No matter how carefully censorship was handled at home and in the war zones there were occasional slipups. The Associated Press, for example, pulled one blunder that could have had serious consequences. As the time approached when the Allies planned to invade Europe, a Teletype tape was prepared that would flash the announcement of the landings from London to New York and then to newspaper offices throughout the United States. This tape was approved by the censors for sending on D-Day morning.

By some accident this precut tape was fed into a Teletype machine in the London office of the Associated Press exactly one week before D-Day by a Teletype operator practicing on her machine. Instantly the flash went out, and moments later Teletypes clattered all over the United States with the bulletin: ALLIED TROOPS LAND IN FRANCE! Fortunately, a "kill" bulletin followed this premature announcement within two minutes and no newspapers printed it. It was, however, used on some radio stations, but no real harm was done.

Generally speaking censorship made an enormous contribution to Allied victory in World War II. And in keeping secret one of the truly vital events of the conflict, censorship played an absolutely essential role. This was the manufacture and dropping of the first atom bomb on Japan —a feat that was probably the best kept secret of the war.

XV

The Best Kept Secret of the War

When World War II began, most of the major industrial nations of the world were working on producing energy by scientifically splitting the nucleus or central core of the atom. This process, called *nuclear fission,* was accomplished in 1939 by the Germans at Kaiser Wilhelm Institute in Berlin. By splitting the atom of the radioactive element uranium, which is found in certain rare minerals, enormous amounts of energy were produced. In fact, the reaction obtained by the German scientists indicated that if one pound of uranium underwent fission it would release as much energy as would be released by the burning of several thousand tons of coal or the explosion of nine thousand tons of TNT. Hitler's major interest was in using this explosive energy to produce the ultimate secret weapon—one that would totally destroy Germany's enemies.

There were, however, tremendous problems to overcome between splitting the atom and producing a workable atomic or nuclear bomb. One of the world's great scientists who was already well along the way toward solving many of these problems was Dr. Niels Bohr of Denmark. Bohr's theory on the structure of the atom was used by the German scientists in their experiments, and it eventually led directly to the development of the atomic bomb by the United States. Bohr's theory had first been presented in 1913 when he was just twenty-eight years old.

Bohr was violently opposed to the Nazis. Before they occupied his country Bohr came to the United States and told scientists that the Germans had succeeded in splitting the uranium atom. He then worked for a time with scientists at Princeton University helping them with atomic fission experiments, but when the Germans occupied Denmark he returned there to lead a protest movement against the occupation. But in 1943, threatened with imprisonment and possible execution, Bohr fled to Sweden.

A strong pacifist Bohr had long hoped that nuclear fission would be used for peaceful purposes. In discussions with British Intelligence agents, however, he gradually became convinced that the Germans were intent on using it to produce an atomic bomb that could lead to a Nazi-controlled Europe and perhaps the world. If anyone was to develop an atomic bomb, he wanted it to be the Allies, and in 1943 he fled Sweden in a plane provided by British Intelligence. The flight almost cost Bohr his life. Intelligence agents hid him in a secret compartment in the rear of the small plane's fuselage and his oxygen supply was accidentally disconnected. He recovered quickly after landing, however, and after a brief stay in England he was flown to the United States. In the United States he became a top adviser on what was called the Manhattan Project.

The American Manhattan atomic bomb project—it was named after the Manhattan District of U.S. Army Engineers—had been secretly started in 1942 under Brigadier General Leslie Groves. Huge secret military reservations and manufacturing plants had been established at Pasco, Washington, and Oak Ridge, Tennessee. One of the major needs for large-scale nuclear fission was relatively large amounts of uranium and this was produced along with component parts for atomic bombs at both the Washington and Tennessee reservations. Plutonium, another element needed to produce an atomic bomb, also had to be manufactured at both plants. This was a process that took many months. It also involved many thousands of civilian workers as well as scientists and military personnel. Additional groups of scientists and engineers worked in Chicago, Washington, D.C., and Alamogordo, New Mexico. The most remarkable thing about the entire Manhattan Project was that it was kept so secret that the American public as well as the Japanese literally did not know what it was that hit Japan when the first atomic bombs were dropped.

Secrecy was maintained in two ways. First of all, the people who worked on the Manhattan Project lived in complete isolation. Many workers were allowed to have their families with them on the Washington and Tennessee reservations, but they were otherwise cut off from the outside world for the duration of the war. These communities were, of course, self-sufficient as far as food, recreation, and other necessities were concerned, but the workers within them were not allowed to communicate with people outside the project in case they might accidentally divulge the nature of the work. Occasionally, new workers would have to be hired, and when this was done the new workers were only told as much as was absolutely essential about the end results of their particular role in the project.

Because of the secret nature of these reservations numerous stories grew up about them in surrounding communities. Most frequently the stories had to do with the possibility of poison gas being manufactured in them, or that some kind of germ warfare devices were being tested. U.S. Intelligence allowed these stories to spread without contradiction.

The second way secrecy was maintained was by the

Office of Censorship. Early in 1943 Byron Price alerted all editors and broadcasters with the following message:

The Codes of Wartime Practices for the American Press and American Broadcasters request that nothing be published or broadcast about "new or secret military weapons experiments." In extension of this highly vital precaution, you are asked not to publish or broadcast any information whatever regarding war experiments involving: production or utilization of atom smashing, atomic energy, atomic fission, atomic splitting, or any of their equivalents. The use for military purposes of radium or radioactive materials, heavy water, high voltage discharge equipment, cyclotrons. The following elements or any of their compounds: polonium, uranium, ytterbium, hafnium, protactinium, radium, rhenium, thorium, deuterium.

With a few minor exceptions all media followed this directive to the letter. Even when scientists at the University of Chicago under Enrico Fermi produced the first nuclear chain reaction (an essential step in the production of an atomic bomb) and tested it, the press and radio maintained a steady silence. Such a bomb—produced under the supervision of J. Robert Oppenheimer—was exploded near Alamogordo, New Mexico, in the summer of 1945.

When the first test bomb was exploded at Alamogordo, however, it was so enormous that people hundreds of miles away began asking questions about an explosion out on the desert. Alamogordo Air Base immediately issued a story saying that an ammunition dump had blown up. This story was generally accepted by the public. In fact editors and broadcasters had grown so accustomed to blacking out atom bomb stories that when the first bombs were dropped on Hiroshima and Nagasaki in Japan in August of

1945 the Office of Censorship received only a few calls asking whether or not the story could now be told. When assured that the whole story could indeed be told—with the exclusion of certain specific details—many reporters and editors said that the public simply would refuse to believe that each of the two bombs on Japan had the explosive power of approximately twenty thousand tons of TNT.

But when news of the Japanese surrender was announced on August 14, 1945, and pictures of the devastation caused by the atomic bombs began to appear in newspapers throughout the world, the public could not help but believe—believe and wonder at this new and awesome force that mankind had released against itself.

Within a matter of days after the end of World War II Byron Price closed the United States Office of Censorship, and the nation's reporters and broadcasters once again began to write and say what they pleased. Price closed the Office of Censorship as a matter of principle. He did not believe censorship had a place in a democracy during peacetime.

It was also not long before the OSS was disbanded. The OSS was not so much closed down as it was allowed to die —with J. Edgar Hoover's and the FBI's blessing. This was not so much a matter of principle as it was one of inter-service rivalry. Hoover had never really reconciled himself to the competition offered the FBI by the OSS. In peacetime he saw the possibility of the OSS taking over the nation's intelligence activities and possibly eliminating the need for the FBI.

This aerial photo shows the size of the area of damage caused by the atomic bomb dropped on Hiroshima.

AP

AP INDICATES AIMING POINT

0   1

Before he resigned as the head of OSS General Donovan wrote a proposal for a new peacetime intelligence agency, pointing out that Allied victory in World War II had been only barely achieved. What, for example, would have happened if Hitler's Vengeance weapons, the V-1 and V-2 rockets, or Japan's balloon bombs had been equipped with atomic warheads? In the future the United States must never again be caught off guard by failing in times of peace to prepare for war.

But Donovan's words fell on deaf ears. By this time President Roosevelt was dead and Harry Truman had assumed the presidency. Sympathetic with Hoover and somewhat suspicious himself of Donovan's OSS "cloak-and-dagger wild men," Truman let Donovan's proposal die—or apparently so. A few years later when it seemed that the nation did indeed need to have a peacetime intelligence organization that operated on an international scale, the Central Intelligence Agency (CIA) was created. It was patterned almost exactly on Donovan's proposal.

The nation had indeed come a long way since the beginning of World War II when "gentlemen did not read other people's mail." Now intelligence activities on a worldwide scale, even in peacetime, were generally an accepted way of life. How to reconcile the secrecy required by such activities and the democratic principles on which the nation was founded remained a continuing and unsolved problem for the United States. Perhaps this was because the cloak-and-dagger men, even in a democratic society, would not die. They might not even fade away—except to reappear in some other guise, perhaps under another name.

An interesting example of this was provided by a famed World War II agent or double agent, no one was ever quite certain which he was, who went by the name of Dr. Richard Sorge. Under the cover of being a German newspaper correspondent, Sorge was a spy for the Soviet Union operating within Japan all during World War II. Late in the war the Japanese broke Sorge's cover and announced that he had been hanged in Sugamo Prison. Allied agents, however, reported Sorge was never hanged but turned into a double agent working for Japan. Several years after the war Sorge was reportedly seen alive in such places as Shanghai, Singapore, Hong Kong, and Macao. By the late 1970s the CIA presumed he was dead. Probably so. But if Dr. Richard Sorge was dead, it was a certainty that from out of the misty world of international espionage another Sorge would appear, or had already appeared, perhaps right within the United States.

Bibliography

Colvin, Ian. *Chief of Intelligence*. London: Victor Gollancz Ltd., 1951.

Downes, Donald. *The Scarlet Thread*. New York: The British Book Centre, 1953.

Farago, Ladislas. *The Game of the Foxes*. New York: David McKay Co., 1971.

Fest, Joachin C. *Hitler*. New York: Harcourt Brace Jovanovich, Inc., 1974.

Ford, Corey. *Donovan of OSS*. Boston and Toronto: Little, Brown and Co., 1970.

Hutton, Clayton. *Official Secret*. New York: Crown Publishers, Inc., 1961.

Kahn, David. *The Codebreakers*. New York: The Macmillan Co., 1967.

Kennedy, Ludovic. *Pursuit: The Chase and Sinking of the Battleship Bismarck*. New York: Pinnacle Books, Inc., 1975.

Koop, Theodore F. *Weapon of Silence*. Chicago: The University of Chicago Press, 1946.

Lochner, Louis P., ed. *The Goebbels Diaries*. New York: Doubleday & Co., Inc., 1948.

Longmate, Norman. *The G.I.'s in Britain, 1942–1945*. New York: Charles Scribner's Sons, 1975.

McCormack, Donald. *The Master Book of Escapes*. New York: Franklin Watts, Inc., 1975.

———. *The Master Book of Spies*. New York: Franklin Watts, Inc., 1976.

Marshall, Bruce. *The White Rabbit*. Boston: Houghton Mifflin Co., 1953.

Masterman, J. C. *The Double-Cross System in the War of 1939 to 1945*. New Haven and London: Yale University Press, 1972.

Mikesh, Robert C., *Japanese World War II Balloon Bomb Attacks on North America*. Washington, D.C.: Smithsonian Institution Press, 1944, 1977.

Morison, Samuel Eliot. *The Two-Ocean War*. Boston and Toronto: Little, Brown & Co., 1963.

Payne, Robert. *The Life and Death of Adolf Hitler*. New York and Washington: Praeger Publishers, 1973.

Rhodes, Anthony. *Propaganda, The Art of Persuasion: World War II*. New York and London: Chelsea House Publishers, 1976.

Saunders, Hilary St. George. *Combined Operations*. New York: The Macmillan Co., 1943.

Snyder, Louis L. *The War of 1939–1945*. New York: Julian Messner, Inc., 1960.

Speer, Albert. *Inside the Third Reich*. New York: The Macmillan Co., 1970.

Stevenson, William. *A Man Called Intrepid*. New York and London: Harcourt Brace Jovanovich, 1976.

Sweets, John F. *The Politics of Resistance in France, 1940–1944*. DeKalb: Northern Illinois University Press, 1976.

Thorpe, Elliott R., Brig. Gen. *East Wind, Rain*. Boston: Gambit Inc., 1969.

Toland, John. *The Rising Sun*, 2 vols. New York: Random House, 1970.

Webber, Bert. "The Bombing of North America." *American History Illustrated*, Gettysburg, Pa., December 1976.

Winterbotham, F. W. *The Ultra Secret*. New York, Evanston, San Francisco, and London: Harper & Row, 1974.

Index

About the Author

Don Lawson, author of 18 books for young people, served with the United States Air Force's counterintelligence office during World War II. After the war, Mr. Lawson joined *Compton's Encyclopedia,* where he eventually became editor in chief. He then joined United Educators, publishers of *American Educator's Encyclopedia,* where he is presently editor in chief.

Don Lawson and his wife, Bea, make their home in Chicago, Illinois.

DISCARDED